The Protectionist
Threat to Corporate
America

Recent Titles from Quorum Books

U.S. Commercial Opportunities in the Soviet Union: Marketing, Production, and Strategic Planning Perspectives
Chris C. Carvounis and Brinda Z. Carvounis

An Analysis of the New Financial Institutions: Changing Technologies, Financial Structures, Distribution Systems, and Deregulation
Alan Gart

The Commercialization of Outer Space: Opportunities and Obstacles for American Business
Jonathan N. Goodrich

Computer Power and Legal Language: The Use of Computational Linguistics, Artificial Intelligence, and Expert Systems in the Law
Charles Walter, editor

Direct Marketing, Direct Selling, and the Mature Consumer: A Research Study
James R. Lumpkin, Marjorie J. Caballero, and Lawrence B. Chonko

The Ethics of Organizational Transformation: Mergers, Takeovers, and Corporate Restructuring
W. Michael Hoffman, Robert Frederick, and Edward S. Petry, Jr., editors

Cable TV Advertising: In Search of the Right Formula
Rajeev Batra and Rashi Glazer, editors

The Marketer's Guide to Selling Products Abroad
Robert E. Weber

Corporate Social Responsibility: Guidelines for Top Management
Jerry W. Anderson, Jr.

Product Life Cycles and Product Management
Sak Onkvisit and John J. Shaw

Human Resource Management in the Health Care Sector: A Guide for Administrators and Professionals
Amarjit S. Sethi and Randall S. Schuler, editors

Export Strategy
Subhash C. Jain

The Protectionist Threat to Corporate America

THE U.S. TRADE DEFICIT AND MANAGEMENT RESPONSES

Louis E. V. Nevaer and
Steven A. Deck

Q

QUORUM BOOKS
NEW YORK · WESTPORT, CONNECTICUT · LONDON

HF
1014
N53
1989

Library of Congress Cataloging-in-Publication Data

Nevaer, Louis E. V.
The protectionist threat to corporate America : the U.S. trade deficit and management responses / Louis E. V. Nevaer and Steven A. Deck.
p. cm.
Includes index.
ISBN 0-89930-363-3 (lib. bdg. : alk. paper)
1. Balance of trade—United States. 2. United States—Commercial policy. 3. Free trade and protection—Protection. 4. Competition, International. I. Deck, Steven A. II. Title.
HF1014.N53   1989
382. 1'7'0973—dc19   88-39910

British Library Cataloguing in Publication Data is available.

Library of Congress Catalog Card Number: 88-39910
ISBN: 0-89930-363-3

First published in 1989 by Quorum Books

Greenwood Press, Inc.
88 Post Road West, Westport, Connecticut 06881

Printed in the United States of America

∞™

The paper used in this book complies with the Permanent Paper Standard issued by the National Information Standards Organization (Z39.48-1984).

10 9 8 7 6 5 4 3 2 1

Copyright Acknowledgments

The publisher and authors are grateful to the following for granting use of their material:

Reprinted by permission of the *Harvard Business Review*. An excerpt from "Tailored Trade: Dealing with the World as It Is" by Pat Choate and Juyne Linger, January-February 1988. Copyright © 1988 by the President and Fellows of Harvard College; all rights reserved.

Figure 4.2 and Tables 1.1 and 4.1 are from *World Development Report, 1987* (New York: Oxford University Press). Courtesy of The World Bank.

Nora Astorga
Presente

≫

CONTENTS

≫

ILLUSTRATIONS

Figures

Tables

≫

ACKNOWLEDGMENTS

Es justo que con este, el tercer libro, se reconozca el apoyo que se ha recibido y por lo tanto se da las gracias a doña Raquel Romero de B., a don Salvador Barajas Manzano, y, a doña María de la Cruz Segura.

É molto importante a riconoscere e ringraziare la mia famiglia e gli amici per la loro ispirazione e il loro supporto di me per il mio sforzo durante gli anni, piu notevolmente i miei genitori, Howard C. e Antonia Deck, e il mio fratello, Dott. Walter J. Deck.

It is also important to acknowledge the support of friends who have inspired this work but who have died during the writing of this book: Nora Astorga, Hector Banda, Louise Nevelson, Linda Sarnoff, and Andy Warhol.

INTRODUCTION

The world trade that is responsible for global economic growth is now threatened by a resurgence of protectionist sentiment. The United States sustained unparalleled economic growth since the Second World War that made it a world power based on a program that encouraged and rewarded international trade. Not only were trade policies designed to restore the shattered economies of our allies, but these also made economic sense. The lesson that trade, as David Ricardo first demonstrated in 1817, enriches the domestic economies of the trading nations was not lost. The establishment of the Bretton Woods system following the conclusion of the war set in motion a series of policies that promoted trade, allowed for economic recovery of the Western nations and Japan, encouraged American exports, and made the United States the political and economic leader of the Western world.

The emergence of protectionist sentiment in the United States in the wake of the accumulation of several years of record-breaking trade deficits poses a danger to future economic growth. World trade, despite the progress made through GATT (General Agreement on Tariffs and Trade), is endangered. This book discusses the implications of protectionism on the U.S. and world economies. As the new administration begins to establish policies that will affect and shape the economy as the twenty-first century dawns, it is imperative for members of the business community to grasp the underlying principles governing inter-national trade and the consequences of protectionism. The is-sues are complex, yet there is no other alternative but to master the basic principles. The simplistic arguments offered by pro-ponents of trade restrictions are very misleading.

The argument made by John Stuart Mill in his *Principles of Political Economy*, first published in 1848, bears repeating today:

From this exposition we perceive in what consists of the benefit of international exchange, or in other words, foreign commerce. Setting aside its enabling countries to obtain commodities which they could not produce themselves at all; its advantage consists in a more effi-cient employment of the productive forces of the world. If two coun-tries which trade together attempted, as far as was physically possible, to produce for themselves what they now import from one another, the labor and capital of the two countries would not be so productive, the two together would not obtain from their industry so great a quantity of commodities, as when each employs itself in producing, both for itself and for the other, the things in which its labor is rela-tively most efficient. The addition thus made to the produce of the two combined, constitutes the advantage of trade.[1]

The advantage of trade, as Mill noted, lies in its ability to dis-tribute efficiently productive functions among nations. Brazil's ability to funnel resources into coffee production, for example, benefits consumers in Texas where coffee is consumed but not produced. In return, Texans can produce oil, which is shipped to Brazil where it is scarce. Thus, each partner concentrates on its relative strengths for the benefit of both trading partners.

The assumption on which the existing world economy is built is that trading partners benefit when each specializes in pro-ducing those commodities that they are able to produce effi-ciently relative to the other trading partners. The discussion presented in this book centers on teaching corporate officers enough about the theoretical fundamentals of trade economics to understand how economic growth can be undermined by protectionist legislation. In addition the timing of this book could not be better: the new administration must address the trade deficit. The discussion presented will allow business people to transcend political rhetoric and understand the core issues involved. This will enhance corporate America's ability to grasp the threat posed by a resurgence in protectionist sentiment.

However well intentioned proponents of protectionist measures may be, their policy recommendations are misguided. One of the most important legacies of the Reagan administration is the resolve to resist pressures to encourage protectionism. While there are notable exceptions, such as quotas for textiles and voluntary export restraints on Japanese car manufacturers, on the whole, the Reagan administration strengthened GATT and promoted trade. This progress, however, is endangered if further gains are not made. The words of Mill must be remembered, especially in a time when there is a redistribution of economic and political power among the Western democracies. In many ways, those calling for protectionism seek to restore the world as it was immediately following the Second World War. Such nostalgic motives are naïve in nature and doomed to backfire.

For this reason it is imperative that corporate executives understand the underlying dynamics of the issue of trade. As the century draws to a close, the heightened competitiveness of the international marketplace will intensify. If corporate America is to hold its ground and stage a comeback in key markets it will do so only through a program that enables America's competitiveness to meet the global challenges. Indeed, if the economic dislocation of recent years is to be arrested, corporate officers must focus on their strengths, acquire a sustainable competitive advantage, adopt a more dynamic management style, and harness the benefits of economies of scale and scope.

The discussion presented in this book constitutes a blueprint that guides the corporate manager through the fundamental issues of trade. The dilemma of trade is crucial to understanding the powerful dynamics under which the world operates today. It is vital that every executive officer have a thorough understanding of the principles of trade, of how power influences trade, and of how trade relations are, in essence, power relations. From this perspective the entire issue of trade takes on a more precise dimension. It provides the corporate officer with a firm foundation on which to implement the four-point program capable of reversing the recent economic dislocation, which has eroded America's leadership position in the world community.

The corporate executive must implement strategies that address the problems of low productivity and lack of competitiveness, which are fundamental in resolving the dilemma of trade from a position of strength. The complexities of the global marketplace leave no room for a halfhearted resolve to the tasks at hand. This is not to say that the challenges the corporate community faces are overwhelming. On the contrary, as the two case studies—one in the service sector, the other in the high-tech field—show, the emphasis must lie on the identification of opportunities, and on sound strategies for exploiting these opportunities. The recent resurgence in the manufacturing sector of the nation's economy demonstrates how a more reasonable exchange rate can encourage exports. While the utility of revaluations has its limits, and its dangers, such as inflation, the need for long-term sustainable exchange rates and cooperation on an international level among the Western democracies is vital if the kind of stability required for growth is to be established. The United States faces many challenges as it develops a sound program that will encourage a renaissance in corporate America's stature in the world, for only then will Mill's "benefit of international exchange" be fully realized.

NOTE

1. John Stuart Mill, *Principles of Political Economy*, vol. 2 (New York: P. F. Collier and Son, 1900), p. 96.

PART I

The Dilemma of Trade

THE NATURE OF TRADE

Trade is the foundation on which the modern world is built. It is the flow of goods and services among nations that is meant when one refers to "the global economy." No matter how elusive that phrase may be at times, it is the best way of grasping an abstract concept. The idea behind trade—and the logical extension of that thought to world trade, and hence, a world economy—lies behind the economic integrity of the world in which we live.

Nations trade. This trade creates an interdependency that constitutes a global economy among the trading partners. In any discussion of trade, therefore, it is necessary to address why the world economy is based on the interdependency trade fosters. Indeed, trade in the postmodern world is inevitable. It is precisely this inevitability of trade that requires a thorough discussion of the nature of trade, the U.S. role in the world economy, and the threat protectionism poses to our welfare. Why trade in the modern world is inevitable is of crucial importance. Nations that close their doors to the world become isolated, backward, and suffer significant declines in the standard of living of their citizens. Aside from an extreme case, for most of the world's nations trade is inevitable.

THE INEVITABILITY OF TRADE

Nations trade because they have no choice but to trade. The country that chooses to shut itself off from the world, such as Albania, is impoverished as a result. The undeniable fact that nature has not distributed resources equally among nation-states means that it is necessary to trade in order to exchange what is plentiful for what is rare. Saudi Arabia, blessed with oil, exchanges its oil for money in order to buy food, which is rare. New Zealand trades its wool for computers. Mexico exchanges tourist services to secure the money necessary to purchase advanced technology. Each nation tries to sell what it has that others need and to buy what others have that it requires. Each nation tries to benefit from its natural resources that constitute a natural competitive advantage (Table 1.1).

Describing the benefits of trade, however, does not explain why it is inevitable. Trade among nations is inevitable for two reasons. The first of these is that almost no nation is self-sufficient in all resources in the quantities it wants, and the second is that citizens of one nation may desire commodities produced elsewhere because they are of superior quality, better value, or scarce in their own nation. Nations trade, then, to secure resources that are plentiful elsewhere or because the kinds of products they desire are made in other nations at a better price or higher quality. If a nation chooses to close itself off from the rest of the world, it suffers. Albania is a fine example of this. This tiny nation, nestled between Yugoslavia and Greece, has only a handful of embassies in other countries and does not belong to the United Nations or any other international organization. It has a backward economy, one of the lowest standards of living in the whole of Europe, and there is almost no contact with foreigners. Albania is the poorer for its decision to refuse to trade.

For the rest of the world, however, contact and trade are inevitable because they increase the number of options for each nation. The exchange of what is plentiful in natural resources and human talents for desired products increases commerce, creates jobs, facilitates access to technologies and markets, and enhances the flow of ideas and knowledge among nations.

Table 1.1
Percentage Share of Merchandise Exports of Selected Countries

Country	Fuels, minerals, and metals		Other primary commodities		Machinery and transport equipment		Textiles and clothing		Other manufactures	
	1965	1985	1965	1985	1965	1985	1965	1985	1965	1985
Canada	28	22	35	17	15	40	1	1	21	20
West Germany	7	5	5	7	46	47	5	5	37	36
Hong Kong	2	2	11	6	6	24	43	32	38	36
Japan	2	1	7	1	31	62	17	3	43	33
Korea, Rep. of	15	4	25	5	3	36	27	23	29	32
Nicaragua	4	2	90	85	-	-	-	1	6	12
Saudi Arabia	98	98	1	-	1	1	-	-	1	1
United States	8	8	27	17	37	48	3	2	25	25

Source: World Bank, World Development Report 1987, pp. 222–223.

Corporate America is given the advantage of unlimited opportunities through liberal trade policies. Access to foreign markets and the ready availability of foreign products stand to benefit firms that can take advantage of trade to increase market share, realize handsome profits, and create growth for this nation's economy. Whether or not American firms have been successful in taking advantage of these opportunities is another matter.

Although trade is inevitable, the dismal trade figures of the 1980s have revealed that during this time corporate America failed to meet the challenges it faced, was not able to enhance its position in the world economy, and suffered important defeats at the hands of foreign competition (Figure 1.1). This inability to compete resulted in an important devaluation of the U.S. dollar, which failed to reverse the tide. While the trade figures have improved, the trade deficit of late 1988 was at a high level in a historic context—and it came at a high price, a lower standard of living that accompanies any devaluation. The national economy is now threatened by the protectionist sentiment of would-be saviors. For the corporate officer the turbulence is disturbing: one year the dollar's strength prices American goods out of world markets, the next a steep devaluation results in great confusion as unstable exchange rates erode confidence in the U.S. economy.

The absence of stability in the foreign exchange markets aggravates the task of the corporate officer. As strategic policies are designed and implemented, forces outside the control of the firm threaten to undermine the most careful execution of corporate plans. The importance of restoring corporate America's international competitiveness has been the topic of great interest in recent years. The arguments presented here contribute to the national debate on trade, protectionism, and the nature of the opportunities and threats faced by corporate America, but differ from other literature in a fundamental way. We contend that modern trade relations are *power* relations. Thus the outcome of any round of trade talks and negotiations depends on the power positions of the parties involved. The discussion presented here, then, assumes that trade, commerce, and international business take place in the real world.

Figure 1.1
U.S. Merchandise Trade Balance 1980–1987

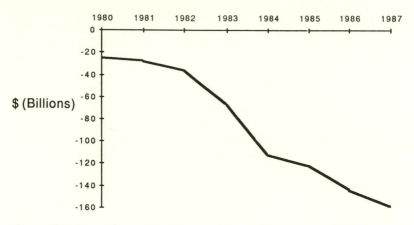

Source: U.S. Department of Commerce, Bureau of Economic Analysis, U.S. International Transactions Accounts.

This is not to say that the theories economists have devised to explain economic forces are not important. They are vital to understanding international trade. At the same time, however, a theoretical explanation that fails to incorporate how human beings interact falls short of the task at hand. The nature of trade is very much tied to the nature of humans. To understand trade one needs to understand human nature. In the world of business the closing of the deal, the agreement to exchange a given good for a given price, and the compliance with contractual obligations are all social interactions inherent in the normal operation of business. Trade is the collective business activities of nations with other nations. How trade is conducted, how nations behave, and what economic decisions businesses make reflect the culmination of complex social interactions among humans. If the corporate officer expects to gain insight into the nature of trade, a thorough understanding of how humans interact is necessary. To this end, the reader must understand how collective rationality differs from individual rationality.

The decision an individual alone makes is not always the same choice he would make if he conferred with another individual. The reason for this is that what is a rational choice for an individual is not necessarily the rational choice for a group of individuals. In *Micromotives and Macrobehavior* Thomas Schelling describes a paradox familiar to most Americans. Individual hockey players almost never choose to wear a helmet; yet when asked, most individual hockey players agree that there should be rules requiring all hockey players to wear helmets. The reason for the discrepancy between individual choice and what is deemed beneficial for the collective is plain to see. Hockey players want to win as much as they want to be protected against injury. Because no matter how slight, wearing helmets reduces visibility to a degree, and thereby affects performance. An individual hockey player would be at a disadvantage if he freely chose to wear a helmet. For the individual the rational choice is to forego the helmet in order to maintain his maximum performance. The cost of protecting his individual peak performance, however, is the incurment of greater risk. The absence of rules to the contrary, however, results in a player's decision to seek a competitive advantage over his opponent by not wearing a helmet. The other individuals on his team and on the opposing team face the same circumstances and the same options. Thus each hockey player decides not to wear a helmet even though each player acknowledges that there should be rules requiring everyone to wear a helmet.[1]

TRADE AS A PRISONER'S DILEMMA

In the absence of an agreement, or a rule, the individual rationality each player adopts results in a radically different outcome than if the players cooperated beforehand and agreed that every player should wear a helmet. The discrepancies between individual and collective rationality can be seen best in what is called the "Prisoner's Dilemma" by social scientists. (Economists treat such discrepancies among consumers as stated vs. revealed preference, for as behaviorists teach, actions speak louder than words.)

The prisoner's dilemma offers insights into how the collective outcome is shaped by the individual choices the partici-

Figure 1.2
The Prisoner's Dilemma

PRISONER A

	Does Not Confess	Confesses
Does Not Confess	Prisoner A: 1 Year Jail Term Prisoner B: 1 Year Jail Term	Prisoner A: Set Free Prisoner B: 20 Year Jail Term
Confesses	Prisoner A: 20 Year Jail Term Prisoner B: Set Free	Prisoner A: 3 Year Jail Term Prisoner B: 3 Year Jail Term

PRISONER B

pants face. The classic prisoner's dilemma example concerns the capture by the police of two criminals who are separated into different cells and questioned individually. Both prisoners, A and B, are guilty and each is told that if he confesses while the other does not then the confessor will be set free while the holdout will go to jail for twenty years. If they both confess then each will receive three years and if neither one confesses then each will go to jail for a year. Neither prisoner is allowed to speak to the other and neither is told what the other one has decided to do. The choices the prisoners face are summarized above (Figure 1.2).

The choices for Prisoner A are straightforward. He can either confess or he can remain silent. If he confesses and Prisoner B also confesses then both prisoners will go to jail for three years. If he confesses and Prisoner B does not confess, then he will go free while Prisoner B is incarcerated for twenty years. Thus if Prisoner A confesses he will either go to jail for three years or he will go free. If Prisoner A does not confess and Prisoner B does confess, then he will go to jail for twenty years and Prisoner B will go free. If Prisoner A does not confess and Prisoner B does not confess either then each will go to jail for one year. Thus, if Prisoner A does not confess he will either go to jail for twenty years or one year. The individual rational choice for Prisoner A is to confess. If he confesses the worst he can do is to go to jail for three years, but if he is lucky he may go free. Prisoner A will confess.

The same rationale is true for Prisoner B. He, too, will confess. Thus the collective outcome is that both prisoners confess and they both go to jail for three years. This collective outcome, however, is suboptimal. It would have been better for both prisoners to cooperate, remain silent, and receive only one-year sentences. The collectively rational choice is to remain silent—but the challenge, however, is how to achieve this result. The only way for the optimal collective outcome to prevail would be for both prisoners to agree *before* their arrest that they would refuse to confess. Even if such an agreement had been made, however, unless there is an ethical bond between both prisoners—or some other enforcement mechanism, such as a death threat of sorts that is common among the Mafia—there is no way to ensure that both prisoners would comply with their agreement.

The only way for the collectively optimal choice to prevail would be for a previous agreement to be made between both parties and for an enforcement mechanism to be in place to guarantee compliance. The absence of either an agreement between the prisoners or an enforcement mechanism would result in a collapse of the agreement, a forefeiture of the collectively optimal outcome, and a triumph of individual rationality resulting in a collectively suboptimal outcome. In other words, both prisoners would be worse off than they could otherwise be if they cooperated. Instead of both going to jail for one year, they would each remain behind bars for a total of three years.

The prisoner's dilemma is very enlightening when one tries to understand the complex nature of international trade and the choices nations, as well as firms, face each day in the business world. All economists agree that in a perfect world the optimal collective outcome for all nations would be to allow the free movement of trade across borders. There would be an efficient allocation of resources throughout the world and all consumers would benefit from lower prices and higher disposable incomes. Firms would enjoy growth and be free of government interference. Nations would enjoy stable growth that would be characterized by acceptable inflation, unemployment, and interest rates. This kind of world exists only in the abstract. In the real world, trade among nations is similar to the situation of the hockey players: while each player concedes that they would all be better off if each player were required to wear a helmet, each player chooses not to do so in order to gain a competitive advantage on those few, seemingly foolish players who do, indeed, wear helmets. The prisoner's dilemma characterizes the choices faced by both nations and hockey players.

Thus our first observation about the nature of trade emerges: *In the absence of an enforcement mechanism, trade agreements among nations will not result in the preservation of the optimal collective outcome in and of themselves.*

Each nation, striving to look after its own interests, will not cooperate when there is no guarantee that the negotiated agreement will be complied with by the signing parties. This is why the United States imposes restrictions on textile imports from Brazil and the Caribbean operates in defiance of the principles of free trade and why the Japanese allow untrue television broadcasts warning Japanese consumers to avoid California produce because it is contaminated with pesticides that cause birth defects in babies. Each nation, like each hockey player or prisoner, makes a decision it knows is in its individual, although not collective, interest. The result in each case is a suboptimal collective outcome: American and Japanese consumers are worse off, hockey players suffer head and dental injuries, and both prisoners spend more time in jail than they would have otherwise.

The dilemma of free trade is real and the costs are reflected, for example, in higher consumer prices, inefficient resource allocation among nations, or impoverished business communities that cannot benefit from the world markets available for their products. In addition, nations are denied the tax revenues that greater economic activity would generate. But while the dilemma of free trade is real, it would be wrong to characterize world trade as chaotic and without agreements. Many of the rules of GATT are respected and treaties among nations are complied with by the respective parties. There is a wide system of cooperation among trading partners. Indeed, the recent American-Canadian free trade zone agreement and the splendid success of the European Economic Community are fine examples of nations resisting the urge of individual rationality for the greater benefits of collective rationality. There is much to say for negotiations that result in the optimal collective outcome prevailing among all parties.

TRADE RELATIONS AS POWER RELATIONS

The success of collective rationality over individual rationality is based on a phenomenon that is curiously absent in the literature today. Most writings on trade discuss the economics of trade or the legislative process by which governments reach accords on trade. This discussion, however, examines trade relations as power relations. The manner in which nations trade with each other and how the benefits of trade are divided between the trading partners is as much a result of power relations as anything else. Max Weber, the nineteenth-century German political scientist and sociologist, defined power as "the possibility of imposing one's will on the behavior of [others]."[2] Indeed, trade relations among nations are in many ways a game of wills in which, through superior gamesmanship or outright economic-political strength, there is one clear victor. Although this is more true of trade relations between weaker and stronger nations than between nations of similar status, the underlying power struggle is there nonetheless.

Trade, for the purposes of this discussion, can—and should—

be seen as the positioning of terms under which there is an exchange of goods and services. The economic dislocation of the past decade in the minds of many observers reveals a disturbing transfer of power from the United States to its major trading partners. The United States is, in effect, losing power. The American economy, now threatened by domestic deficits and persistent trade deficits, poses serious challenges for today's manager. The deterioration of the American status in the world economy diminishes the ability of American firms to compete in the global economy.

The assumption alluded to here is that the economic dislocation the United States has suffered during the past decade reveals a loss of economic and political power. In terms of trade the United States has been weakened at the bargaining table. Thus it is no longer in a position to impose "one's will upon the behavior" of others. In turn America today increasingly seeks the comfort of protectionism to deny this obvious fact. Trade, which is the lifeblood of the world economy, can be readily undermined by protectionist legislation that invites retaliation. The closing of markets would make a difficult task almost impossible for the corporate officer.

There is a certain degree of cooperation that is implied in the characterization of trade as lifeblood. Whether trade will flow freely depends on the kinds of agreements into which governments enter. And the kinds of agreements a nation will enter into depend on its relative position vis-à-vis other nations. The prisoner's dilemma demonstrates that there is an optimal collective outcome to be achieved through negotiations that are guaranteed by enforcement mechanisms. These enforcement mechanisms, moreover, can be either punitive penalties for violating the agreement or an ethical understanding that will not be violated by the signing parties. There is, however, an unspoken assumption in the prisoner's dilemma. That is, both parties are assumed to be of equal rank. The hockey players of both teams are in the same league and the prisoners were partners in crime. In both cases, the members who are in agreement, or wish they were, are equals. The most successful trade agreements are likewise among nations of equal power. The members of Europe's Common Market are all democracies that respect each other and have comparable standards of living and per capita GNPs. The United States and Canada are both first-world nations with high standards of living and sophisticated economies.

For these nations it is easy to negotiate the optimal collective outcome. On the other hand, the nature of trade as power suggests that when unequal nations negotiate trade agreements, the notion that both nations will be better off is not to be taken for granted. In the continuing disagreements between the United States and Brazil over the trade of software, for example, the unequal economic power of these nations, coupled with comparable levels of social and political power, makes negotiation difficult. The free trade notion that Brazil would benefit from free trade is not as self-evident as Milton Freidman would have us believe. For decades leftist economists have written on "dependency" theory, which argues that when underdeveloped nations allow free trade, the more powerful nations come to dominate their economies, rendering them dependent on the larger nations, thus impoverishing the weaker nations.

There is undeniable empirical evidence to support this theory. The problem for us, moreover, is that the state of economic thought today is not sufficiently advanced to help us understand the problems of development. Few nations have been able to develop using free trade and this failure poses problems for future development. The nature of this problem, however, is tied in to the nature of trade. The lack of economic theories that promote development in the real world, coupled with the undeniable lopsided nature of trade between the poor and rich countries, poses problems for corporate America as the United States begins a major campaign to restore its competitiveness in the world economy. The reason for this is that trade and power are very much interlinked and cannot be separated from each other.

Thus our second observation about the nature of trade emerges: *Trade relations are power relations in which two nations of unequal status will find it difficult to negotiate an outcome that benefits both equally and that does not result in the creation of a dependency of one nation on the other.*

NOTES

1. Thomas Schelling, *Micromotives and Macrobehavior* (New York: W. W. Norton, 1978), p. 68.

2. Max Weber, *Max Weber on Law in Economy and Society* (Cambridge: Harvard University Press, 1954), p. 323.

THE DILEMMA OF TRADE

An individual nation faces the same dilemma as an individual hockey player. The prisoner's dilemma for the hockey player is between wearing or not wearing a helmet. There is a very real trade-off involved: competitive advantage or risk. As demonstrated, barring an agreement that is guaranteed by an enforcement mechanism, the individual hockey player will ultimately choose not to wear a helmet. Thus, the absence of an enforceable agreement between the players results in a suboptimal outcome: While an individual hockey player is in favor of all players wearing helmets, because there is no such requirement he cannot, in good conscience, incur a handicap that will reduce his effectiveness, and he thereby foregoes a helmet.

The prisoner's dilemma nations face is between restricting or not restricting trade. Not unlike the hockey player, an individual nation exercising prudence will end up in a suboptimal outcome when enforceable agreements are absent. Consider the following scenario every nation faces: Should trade be restricted or not? There are only two possible choices, yes or no. To make things simple, consider a world in which there are only two nations, A and B. (A more complex world has Nation A and All Other Nations.) Nation A is faced with two choices. It can either trade freely or it can restrict trade. Nation B faces the same options. Therefore Nation A has to consider Nation B's decision when deciding what it will do. In order to determine what the prudent decision is, Nation A needs to rank the four possible outcomes in this dilemma.

The first best world for Nation A is one in which it restricts trade while Nation B does not. In this manner Nation A protects its domestic economy while having access to the domestic economy of Nation B. Nation A will be at a marked advantage for it enjoys access to foreign markets while protecting its domestic producers. This is clearly the best possible world for Nation A—even though it is unfair to Nation B.

The second best world for Nation A is one in which both nations allow free trade. Nation A would enjoy access to Nation B's markets and Nation B would have access to Nation A's domestic market. Although its domestic economy is no longer protected, the opportunity to trade abroad, expand markets, and let the fittest firms survive more than compensates for opening up the domestic market. In addition, by allowing Nation B to sell in its domestic economy, Nation A makes sure that its domestic producers remain competitive and its domestic consumers enjoy lower prices and a higher standard of living.

The third best world for Nation A would be for both nations to restrict trade. Even though Nation A would be denied access to Nation B's domestic markets, it would not be required to open its own markets to the producers of Nation B. It is clear that both nations are worse off for not trading—which is one reason why this is Nation A's third choice—but of equal consideration is the protection of domestic producers.

The least best world for Nation A is the final possible outcome: Nation A has no access to Nation B's domestic economy, but Nation B is allowed to have a presence in Nation A's domestic markets. This outcome is the opposite of Nation A's first choice. The circumstances are reversed. Whereas before Nation A had access to Nation B's economy while protecting its own domestic market, now Nation B can profit while not reciprocating accessibility.

Nation A's preference ranking is represented in Figure 2.1. The other party to this dilemma, Nation B, faces precisely the same reasoning as Nation A. Its own ranking of the possible outcomes is the same as that of Nation A and for the same

Figure 2.1
The Dilemma of Trade

NATION A

	Unrestricted Trade	Restricted Trade
Unrestricted Trade	Nation A: 2nd Best Outcome Nation B: 2nd Best Outcome	Nation A: 1st Best Outcome Nation B: 4th Best Outcome
Restricted Trade	Nation A: 4th Best Outcome Nation B: 1st Best Outcome	Nation A: 3rd Best Outcome Nation B: 3rd Best Outcome

NATION B

Source: International Credit Monitor.

reasons. Nation B's preference ranking is also represented in Figure 2.1. The question now turns to which of the four possible outcomes will prevail. This depends on the nature of the discussions these nations have. In a world resembling our own, we can assume there is little willingness of either nation to sacrifice sovereignty by agreeing to comply with the rulings of a third party. Neither Nation A nor Nation B can be expected to allow an international board of arbitration to rule over what it may, at some point, consider a matter of national security. Therefore, we can safely assume that, while agreements may exist, neither nation will be willing to submit to the rulings of an international arbitration committee or an independent judicial body.

It would seem reasonable to expect each nation to follow a prudent course of action that ensures that its own self-interests are looked after. Now we can understand what the inevitable outcome will be. Nation A is still faced with two choices: trade or restrict trade. From its own rankings of the possible outcomes, it is clear to see that if it decides to restrict trade, it will end up in either its first best world or its third best world, depending on the decision of Nation B. At the same time, should Nation A decide to allow unrestricted trade, it will end up in either its second best or least best outcome, depending again on Nation B's decision. The inevitable choice for Nation A is to avoid running the risk of ending up with the least best outcome and doing all it can to ensure that it may even end up in its first best world. Therefore Nation A will restrict trade. It's a better bet and it's the prudent choice.

Nation B faces the same options and reasons and will also restrict trade. Thus both nations exercise prudent judgment, restrict trade, and end up in a third best possible outcome (Figure 2.2). They may have avoided a least best outcome, but it is clear to see that they are at a suboptimal outcome. Had both nations reached an agreement to allow unrestricted trade they would both have been in their second best possible outcome. This is a clearly superior outcome. Nations fare like individual hockey players it seems. Both default into a third best outcome for lack of an enforcement mechanism that ensures compliance with an agreement. So long as hockey players do not submit to a superior authority they will not wear helmets. So long as nations do not submit to an international enforcement body they will strive to restrict trade.

The dilemma of trade is now self-evident. Nations are not willing to surrender their sovereignty to a third party. This is why institutions such as the United Nations and the World Court lack enforcement powers. No nation is willing to accept orders when it does not suit its own interests. In this present discussion, moreover, the fact that nations default into an inferior outcome through lack of negotiations is at the core of the problems world trade faces today. There are strong pressures in every country to place restrictions on trade. These can range from tariffs to the subsidization of domestic producers to a va-

Figure 2.2
The Dilemma of Trade: Outcome of Two Nations Pursuing Own
Self-Interest

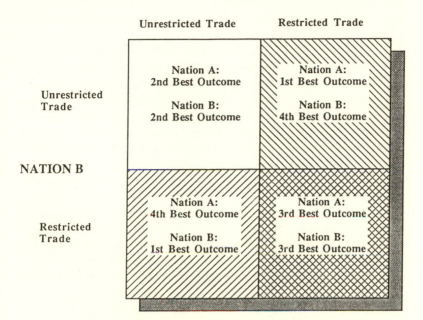

NATION A

Unrestricted Trade   Restricted Trade

| | Nation A: 2nd Best Outcome / Nation B: 2nd Best Outcome | Nation A: 1st Best Outcome / Nation B: 4th Best Outcome |

Unrestricted Trade

NATION B

Restricted Trade

Nation A: 4th Best Outcome / Nation B: 1st Best Outcome

Nation A: 3rd Best Outcome / Nation B: 3rd Best Outcome

Source: International Credit Monitor.

> Left to their own devices, each nation acts in a prudent manner, which results in restricted trade. Nation A chooses to restrict trade, for by so doing it will either end up in its first or third best possible outcome. Nation B faces the same choice. Both nations thus restrict trade, end up in the third best outcome, and forego the optimal outcome.

riety of other measures. No matter which combination of restrictions is designed the result is the same: free trade remains an ideal.

This is not to say that trade doesn't exist, but rather, that even though trade is inevitable in the modern world, it is not allowed to operate without unwarranted interference. The problem with the United States today is that it is not trading as efficiently as it has in the past. It has lost world market shares, domestic producers have been unable to defend effectively the domestic markets, and a net transfer of wealth has taken place, most notably to Japan and West Germany, in the form of enormous balance of trade deficits. The resulting economic dislocation undermines the long-term viability of the American economy and has made the United States dependent on capital inflows to finance current consumption.

The issue of concern in this discussion is to analyze how the United States can improve its ability to compete in the global economy. Implicit in this proposition is how corporate America can make up for lost ground and implement strategic programs that can deliver a sustainable competitive advantage. In the world economy of 1990 this cannot be done without the cooperation of government. In its capacity to legislate the government must ensure that sound trade policies are enacted, that organizations such as GATT (General Agreement on Tariffs and Trade) are strengthened, and that free trade is encouraged. The corporate officer, for his part, must understand the complex nature of trade. Throughout the balance of the book trade theory, economics, and corporate management will be examined to reflect the realities of the prisoner's dilemma that nations and firms face as well as the role of power in shaping which outcome will prevail.

THE ROLE OF POWER AND THE PRISONER'S DILEMMA

Recall the prisoner's dilemma faced by the hockey player. Unless there is a rule requiring all players to wear helmets and there is an enforcement mechanism in place to ensure that all players comply with that rule, then it is the prudent course of action for an individual player not to wear a helmet and thereby incur a competitive disadvantage, even though in private he may prefer to wear a helmet in order to protect his own well-being. The resulting suboptimal outcome reveals that left to their own devices individuals who follow the prudent course of action are collectively worse off than they would otherwise be if cooperation prevailed.

This applies to nations as well. Each nation, following a prudent course of action, will seek to impose restrictions on the trade of other nations. The collective outcome of all these nations' prudent actions is inefficient, but unless there is an enforceable agreement among nations, it is inevitable. In the same manner that the hockey players ended up in a third best world so do nations end up in suboptimal outcomes where trade is concerned. The situation for a hockey player, however, has, in most cases, been rectified. Virtually all leagues now require all players to wear helmets and there are penalties for those who do not comply with the leagues' requirements.

Here, through cooperation born out of common interests, hockey players have ensured that the second best world for an individual player—which is the optimal outcome for all players—prevails. The use of a league as a regulatory body that functions as a guarantor ensures there is no cheating on league rules. The end result is that all players face lower risks of head injuries and none enjoys a competitive advantage from increased visibility.

Nations, however, are not so predisposed to recognize their common interest or work toward the resolution of the dilemma of trade. Part of the reason for this stems from the undeniable fact that some nations are more powerful than others. For the most part all hockey players are equals. While some are better players than others, most leagues are democratic clubs in which all members are afforded equal rights. This is not true for nation-states. Whether it is in economic, military, political, or cultural terms, some nations are more powerful, carry greater clout, and are in positions of greater authority than are other nations. It is not exceptional under these circumstances to find that nations jockey for power positions over each other. Indeed, the words of Max Weber come to mind once again, for, according to him, power is the ability "to realize [one's] will in a communal act against the will of others who are participating in the same act."[1]

The implications for this discussion are clear. The resolution of the dilemma of trade will not automatically be a third best outcome in the absence of an enforceable agreement to the contrary as was the case with the hockey players. The dilemma of trade will be resolved according to the power of the nations concerned. Trade relations are power relations. The outcome that prevails is indicative of this fact. There is, however, some danger in seeing trade relations as remnants of nineteenth century real politik, and it is not our intention to imply that international relations are power struggles as envisioned by Prince Metternich. On the contrary, such "might makes right" arguments fall short of the requirements of the complex world in which we live today. Nevertheless, it must be accepted that power plays an important, albeit unconscious, role in determining the outcome of the dilemma of trade. To see this more clearly, here are some examples of how the United States ends up in all four possible outcomes on nation- or issue-specific trade matters. While the United States enjoys mutually beneficial trade relations with some nations, it cannot be denied that the United States, inevitably, exercises its power over other nations in order to "impose its will." When this occurs, trade is not beneficial to the weaker nation—which is why "development" and "progress" have proven to be such elusive goals for many of the poorer nations of the world.

THE UNITED STATES AND THE CARIBBEAN: FIRST BEST, LEAST BEST OUTCOME

When the United States is in its first best outcome, its reciprocal trading partner is in its least best outcome. This is why critics of the left continue to deplore the "failure" of the free market. The dependency that trade fosters, they claim, impoverishes the weaker nations of the world. As noted, their conclusion is right, but for the wrong reason. If developing nations become dependent because of unrestricted trade, it is because these nations are weaker and are unable to negotiate an optimal outcome to the dilemma of trade. The notion of trade as power interferes with the ability of smaller nations to demand an outcome that is equitable. The stronger nation ends up in its first best outcome and the weaker nation ends up in its least best outcome. No one is denying that the benefits of trade are not evenly divided among the parties, but free trade is not to blame, and neither is a free market economy. The precise conditions under which a weaker nation is forced into a suboptimal outcome to the dilemma of trade are a valid topic to discuss.

To shed light on this process, consider the textile industry in the United States. A labor union official who testified before the House Committee on Energy and Commerce in 1985 for protection legislation against textile imports stated that the "apparel produced in countries with abysmally low living standards and virtually no workers' rights threatens living standards in this country."[2] After much consideration the U.S. government continued its policy of keeping the textile industry one of the most protected industries in this country.

There are significant effects of this legislation designed to restrict the textile trade. For nations that export textiles to the United States the closing of a lucrative market poses difficulties. Nations that export textiles to the United States tend to be Latin American nations in the Caribbean and developing Pacific Rim countries. The export of textiles constitutes a significant source of hard currency for these nations. The "abysmally low living standards" the American trade official complained about will deteriorate even further in the wake of the restricted access to the U.S. market. It is unlikely that the nations affected by the restriction on trade will be in a political or economic position to retaliate against the United States. The net effect, therefore, is that the United States is allowed unrestricted trade with these nations while imposing trade restrictions. The United States will enjoy its first best outcome and the affected nations will end up in their least best position (see Figure 2.3). Trade for the affected nations creates more harm than good for the simple reason that they are not allowed to make the most of an industry in which they have a competitive advantage.

For the American consumer, the result of protectionism is higher costs for clothing. The jobs "saved," if any, come at a high cost. The textile industry claims that between 1980 and 1986 over 350,000 American jobs were lost because of imports. According to Richard McKenzie, however, "productivity increases alone could account for the loss of approximately 225,000 jobs, or 83 percent of the total decrease in employment in the textile industry between 1973 and 1984."[3] The claims that

Figure 2.3
The United States and the Caribbean: First Best, Least Best
Outcome

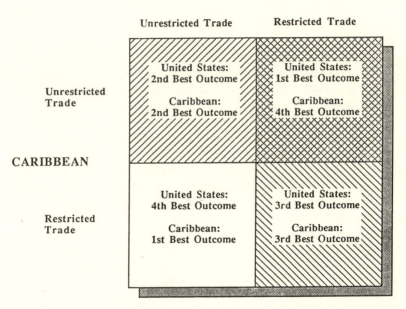

UNITED STATES

Source: International Credit Monitor.

In the real world, power affects trade relations. The United States is more powerful than any Caribbean nation and can therefore "impose its will" on these weaker nations. Its position of power enables the United States to impose the first best outcome from its point of view. Therefore, the United States restricts trade with the Caribbean nations while coercing the Caribbean nations into keeping all markets open to U.S. goods. (Critics of capitalism point to this suboptimal outcome to the dilemma of trade and correctly argue that in cases such as these the weaker nation is impoverished by the dependency the trade and power relations create.)

American jobs must be saved, while weaker countries must give up on one of the few growth industries they enjoy, are tenuous at best. What is important, however, is that this is a case in which the optimal outcome to the dilemma does not prevail. The reason for this lies in the fact that the two nations are not equals.

The implicit coercion power that stronger states can exercise plays a role in determining the dilemma's outcome. Therefore, the United States prevails and the restrictions on trade are imposed. The protection of the domestic textile industry, however, has disruptive effects in both countries. The developing nations, such as those in Latin America, which stand to benefit from increasing their exports to the United States, clearly lose out. While the United States enjoys its first best outcome, the weaker nation is stuck with the least best outcome. Under such circumstances it remains unclear how the countries with "abysmally low living standards" are ever to improve their economic conditions if they are denied access to compete in markets in which they are competitive. For the small nation of Latin America or the Pacific Rim that had expected to benefit from free trade, capture hard currencies, and improve its national economy, the unilateral U.S. decision undermines economic development. The fact that, by definition, weaker nations are powerless to retaliate in measure, means that there are no effective restrictions placed on trade from the United States.

In the long term, however, the weaker nation is not the only one to suffer ill consequences from the restrictions on trade imposed by the United States. America itself stands to pay a high cost for protectionism. "The protection the textile and apparel industry seeks," Richard McKenzie argued, "would not, on balance, save American jobs, nor would it come cheap. . . . It would . . . force consumers to spend an average of $8 billion more a year over the next decade on imported and domestic textile products."[4] Furthermore, the protective measures passed by Congress would cost as many jobs in other industries in the United States as it would save. The distortions that result when markets are insulated are great. While the immediate effect is to please a given constituency, on the whole it is the American consumer who pays the price of protectionism through higher consumer prices and jobs lost through a ripple effect.

The implications for policymakers are clear. In an interdependent world characterized by the globalization of trade, isolated attempts to exercise power over weaker nations have short-term effects. The resolution to the trade dilemma in the textile industry is not satisfactory. While the United States enjoys a first best outcome, it must realize that the benefits are short term. In the final analysis both nations lose. A developing nation is denied access to one of the few markets in which it can compete effectively, thereby dashing hopes of growth (and perhaps need for American foreign aid). The United States consumer is asked to overpay by $8 *billion* for a particular class of consumer goods. The economies of both nations are distorted in the process and on balance there will be a net loss of jobs between both nations. The most important implication of an outcome such as this, however, is that it undermines faith in the free enterprise system. When power determines the outcome of the trade dilemma, the weaker nation is impoverished by free trade, which is hardly a victory in the international community for American ideology.

THE UNITED STATES AND WEST GERMANY: THE OPTIMAL OUTCOME

The optimal outcome to the dilemma of trade prevails when the two nations involved are of equal power. This can be of equal political, military, or cultural power, but in most cases it is a question of equal *economic* power. When two parties are of relative strength, it is easier to negotiate an agreement that acknowledges the benefits of cooperation and the costs of conflict, and promotes the adoption of mutually beneficial solutions to common problems. The complex nature of the trade relations between the United States and West Germany, for example, demonstrates the degree to which there is an ongoing dialogue and cooperation on many levels to ensure that the so-called "level playing field" prevails.

It comes as no surprise, then, to learn that both the United States and West Germany have an enlightened approach to trade. Neither nation attempts to impose undue restrictions on commerce from the other. There are, of course, occasional disagreements on specific issues. This is natural and to be expected in any important human relationship. What remains noteworthy, however, is that the dilemma of trade is resolved in such a way as to allow the best possible outcome to prevail. Both the United States and West Germany negotiate trade agreements that promote unrestricted trade. In this manner they both end up in the second best possible worlds (see Figure 2.4). When nations negotiate with their equals, have respect for each other's sovereignty, and have multifaceted relations, then there is no enforcement mechanism necessary in order to guarantee compliance with the resulting trade agreements.

This does not preclude the emergence of trade disputes. But however many areas of concern arise, the relative equality of their strengths encourages an arbitrated solution that satisfies both parties. The trade relations between the United States and West Germany are, in fact, remarkably unremarkable. The recent strains brought about by a surging dollar and then a surging deutsche mark have been rather minor. Compare the complaints about the flood of West German goods into the United States with all the complaints about Japan's trade surplus with the United States. The discussions about the West German surplus have been much more circumspect. Nations of equal strength recognize problems and discreetly work toward their resolutions. The best diplomacy, after all, takes place behind closed doors and not through headlines in the press of either nation.

Thus, while the economic relations between these two nations have shown a significant absence of hostility, the frustrations accompanying the turbulent behavior of the exchange rates have played themselves out in other arenas. The major points of contention between Washington and Bonn since 1982 have focused on the domestic policies of Bonn. Washington has insisted that Bonn modify its fiscal and monetary policies in order to stimulate the West German economy. The rationale has been a simple one: Washington has maintained that if Bonn were to adopt expansionary domestic policies the West German economy would grow at a faster rate, thereby creating a

Figure 2.4
The United States and West Germany: The Optimal Outcome

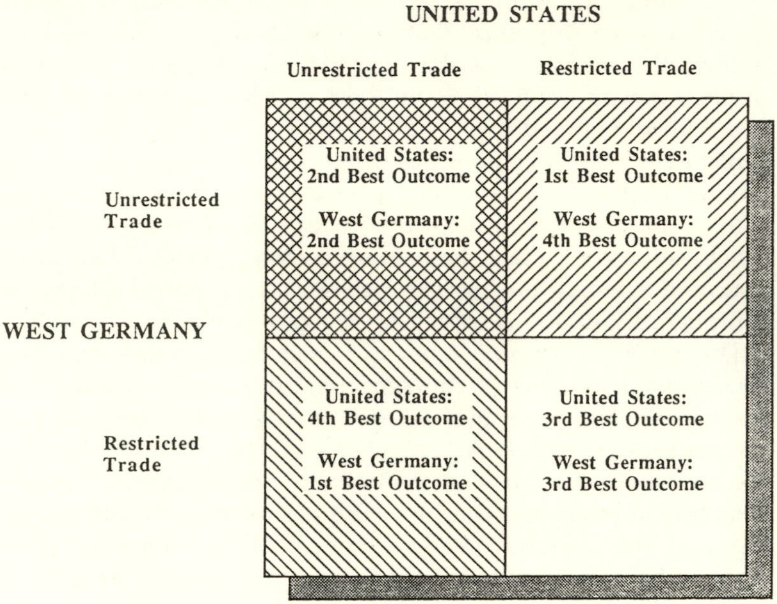

UNITED STATES

	Unrestricted Trade	Restricted Trade
Unrestricted Trade	United States: 2nd Best Outcome West Germany: 2nd Best Outcome	United States: 1st Best Outcome West Germany: 4th Best Outcome
Restricted Trade	United States: 4th Best Outcome West Germany: 1st Best Outcome	United States: 3rd Best Outcome West Germany: 3rd Best Outcome

WEST GERMANY

Source: International Credit Monitor.

In the real world, power affects trade relations. When two nations enjoy relatively equal power, whether political or economic, neither can "impose its will" on the other. In this case both the United States and West Germany realize their own self-interest lies in cooperation. Thus, both nations choose free trade and achieve the best possible outcome to the dilemma of trade.

greater demand for imports—American imports—by the West German consumer. It is the slow growth rate in West Germany, Washington has argued, that exacerbates America's continuing trade deficit with that country.

This point of contention, however, has been ongoing precisely because both nations are relative equals. Unlike a small Caribbean nation, West Germany can hold its own in negotiations with Washington. Thus, an impasse has prevailed in many instances. The West Germans have argued that their domestic policies are their own business and that Bonn has a greater responsibility to its own citizens than to America's. There's nothing unreasonable about such a position. Nevertheless, the dance of the wills has continued. This is as it should be. Washington and Bonn continue in a dialogue of compromise and negotiation.

The net result, however, is important for this discussion. As nations of equal power, the United States and West Germany are not in a position to dictate terms to each other. Both nations realize the tremendous benefits to be gained by cooperation and their trade history reflects this negotiation. The resolution of the dilemma of trade for these two nations is more than satisfactory. Despite recent turbulence in the exchange rates, on the whole both West German and American consumers and businesses are better off than they would otherwise be. The relative power positions of these two nations preclude a cumbersome and expensive enforcement mechanism to ensure compliance with negotiated trade agreements. Under circumstances such as these, the dilemma of trade is not a dilemma at all. The citizens of both nations are enriched by free trade and both nations themselves are made wealthier by free trade. The optimal outcome is a win-win proposition neither party can resist.

THE UNITED STATES AND BRAZIL: A THIRD BEST OUTCOME

There are, however, lose-lose situations as well. The third best outcome is one in which both nations decide to restrict trade or an enforcement mechanism is absent. When this occurs, the worst mutual outcome prevails and both nations are worse off. The fundamental disagreements on trade between the United States and Brazil since the early 1980s demonstrate the disruptive effects the failure to cooperate on trade can have on both nations.

The United States has imposed sanctions on Brazilian imports to this country. These trade restrictions are in retaliation against Brazil's stance on its telecommunications and computer industries. The nature of the continuing dispute between these two nations has fundamental repercussions in the assessment of the role of free trade in the economic development of a nation. The Brazilian position is rather clear. The telecommunications and computer industries are of strategic and national importance to the young nation. If it is to modernize and prepare for the competitive world of the twenty-first century, Brazilian officials maintain, their nation cannot afford to import from foreign nations the technology and know-how that will be used for national security. Therefore, Brazil hopes to develop domestic telecommunications and computer industries that serve the national strategic goals and whose control does not rest in the hands of foreign nationals.

On the surface the Brazilian argument and thinking are sound. After all, the United States itself labels certain industrial domains as being of national security interest and actively regulates developments in firms operating within those industries. When a French firm attempted to acquire Fairchild, for example, the U.S. government blocked the sale until an American firm was found to purchase the troubled company. The logic in the American government's actions was the same as that of the Brazilians: the United States is not prepared to allow control of a firm dealing in an industry with national security implications to be transfered to a foreign firm. No one can deny that sensitive research into advanced microchip technology is of strategic importance, especially in light of the military applications of such technology, and therefore the position of the U.S. government is more than reasonable.

The Brazilians claim that the development of their telecommunications and computer industries is also of a national security nature. For this reason Brazil has refused to modify laws preventing foreign firms from competing for telecommunications contracts or to allow the importation of computer hardware and software. The U.S. position in this affair has been that neither the telecommunications nor computer industries is of military consequence and as such neither industry deserves to be considered from a national security viewpoint. America claims that Brazil's refusal to allow U.S. firms to compete in these industries is an undue interference with free trade and harms the interests of both nations. The failure of diplomatic measures to remedy the situation is one reason the United States has retaliated against Brazilian imports—from textiles to produce to shoes—in order to pressure the Brazilians to reconsider their position on trade.

The dilemma of trade is thus resolved by both parties imposing restrictions on trade that result in a third best outcome (see Figure 2.5). Whether or not the Brazilian stand on the telecommunications and computer industries is proper is not the issue here. The real significance of the continuing disagreements between the United States and Brazil lies in the resolution of the dilemma of trade. Officials in both nations concede in private that the ongoing dispute interferes with their relations and wish the trade problems—which are nothing but a headache—would be quickly resolved. It is clear that the status of trade between Brazil and the United States is unsatisfactory, but there is no clear indication that negotiations will settle the outstanding issues in the near future. The reason for this lies, in part, with the power struggle between these nations. The United States is undeniably the more powerful nation in this dispute. But unlike some small Caribbean, African, or Pacific Rims nations, Brazil is large enough to be able to stand on its own ground. The United States, therefore, is not in a position to dictate terms to Brazil, and since the United States cannot impose its will on Brazil, it must respect Brazilian sovereignty and negotiate.

Here, then, the struggle of two stubborn nations, reluctant to make concessions to each other, results in a default of sorts ending in a third best outcome to the dilemma of trade. The cost of this stubbornness, moreover, is borne by both nations. The American consumer is denied access to Brazilian products that are of high quality at competitive prices. Whether these products are shoes or clothing, the U.S. consumer is encumbered by trade sanctions against Brazil. This results in less competition in the affected industries, higher prices, and lost jobs. Corporate America, likewise, loses out. The tremendous Brazilian domestic market is denied to American firms in the telecommunications and computer industries. Firms such as

Figure 2.5
The United States and Brazil: Third Best Outcome

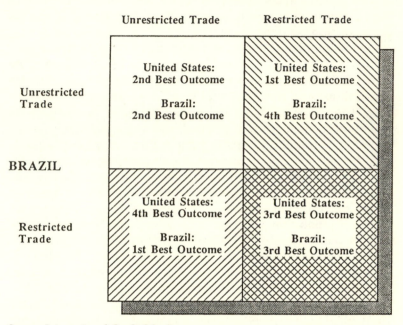

UNITED STATES

Source: International Credit Monitor.

In the real world, power affects trade relations. When two nations enjoy relatively equal power, whether political or economic, neither can "impose its will" on the other. In this case two sovereign nations refuse to cooperate, thus resulting in a third best outcome to the dilemma of trade. Both Brazil and the United States restrict trade. Cooperation would make both nations better off.

AT&T, ITT, IBM, Apple Computer, Digital, and Compaq stand to contribute to Brazilian development if only they were permitted access to the growing Brazilian nation.

The Brazilian consumer is also worse off. The demand for telephone service outstrips supply at present. The wait for the installation of telephone lines is long, telephone equipment is expensive, and the quality of service is substandard. In addition, Brazilian firms lag behind their American counterparts in installing computers to facilitate modernization. If Brazil expects to compete in the next century then it must ensure that its work force is computer literate and that Brazilian firms have implemented extensive computerization programs. In addition, there are countless Brazilian firms that are denied access to the American market. The severe restrictions imposed by the United States against Brazil make it impossible for many capable Brazilian firms to export to the United States. As a result, Brazil's economy does not grow as fast as it could, not as many jobs are created, the Brazilian worker is worse off than he would otherwise be, and Brazil's export earnings suffer, making it more difficult for that nation to service its foreign debt.

The failure of the United States and Brazil to impose their wills on each other, a reluctance to negotiate in earnest toward the resolution of the trade disputes, and the absence of an enforcement mechanism result in the third best outcome prevailing. When trade is restricted in this manner, both nations suffer. The price of refusing to cooperate on trade is very high. The unsatisfactory status of American-Brazilian trade relations indicates that in a more competitive world it is important for two nations who are not in a position to impose their wills on each other to cooperate and construct an enforcement mechanism that ensures compliance with their trade agreements. The irony in the U.S.-Brazil dispute, moreover, lies in the very fact that both American and Brazilian officials show some embarrassment at the very impasse they face. Officials of both nations realize they are hurting themselves as they hurt each other. There are, however, no clear indications that progress will be made in the near future. Therefore it remains an unfortunate fact that two economic giants of the New World have settled for a suboptimal outcome to the dilemma of trade.

THE UNITED STATES AND JAPAN: THE LEAST BEST OUTCOME

There is only one other outcome that is worse than the American-Brazilian standoff. This is when the United States faces trade restrictions in a nation that enjoys complete access to the American market. An outcome such as this is the complete reversal of the situation in the textile industry in which the United States has an advantage over developing nations. As mentioned, this type of unbalanced outcome prevails when the United States, the stronger nation, through the exercise of power, imposes its will on a weaker one. In the aftermath of a decade of progressive economic dislocation, however, the tide has turned against the United States. There are now circumstances under which other nations can exercise leverage over the United States and impose an outcome other nations must endure because of their economic, political, or military weakness. The result is a complete reversal of America's trade relations with the small, weak textile-producing countries (see Figure 2.6).

The trade relations between the United States and Japan reveal the least best outcome for America. The Japanese enjoy complete access to the American markets while the United States is encumbered by a complex labyrinth of restrictions in the domestic Japanese markets. The decade-old dissatisfaction with the status quo between the United States and Japan is now well known. Japan-bashing has been a favorite topic of discussion by politicians and the media alike. The irony of it all, however, lies in the fact that much of the anger against Japan is the result of its remarkable ability to compete in the free market. It must be remembered that Japan gained trade surpluses one sale at a time. Japanese success is the product of more efficient firms capable of responding to and anticipating the needs of the consumer. This, however, is neither here nor there.

What is important for this discussion is to recognize that the Japanese do in fact erect a complex system of nontariff barriers (NTB) that effectively restrict American access to the Japanese domestic market. This situation is further complicated by the Japanese cultural bias against imported goods. The significant price disparities resulting from the stronger yen, however, are changing attitudes as the Japanese consumer realizes that high-quality foreign goods are more reasonably priced than their Japanese-made competition. On balance, however, the situation remains unsatisfactory from America's perspective. The Japanese have ample access to virtually all U.S. domestic markets while American firms face an uphill battle penetrating the domestic Japanese markets.

Figure 2.6
The United States and Japan: Least Best Outcome

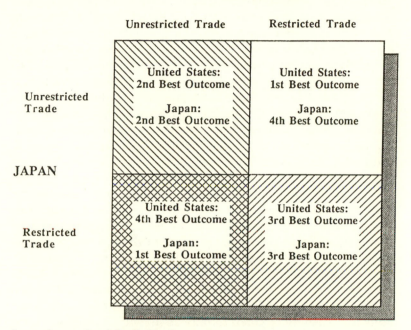

UNITED STATES

Unrestricted Trade | Restricted Trade

Unrestricted Trade

United States:
2nd Best Outcome

Japan:
2nd Best Outcome

United States:
1st Best Outcome

Japan:
4th Best Outcome

JAPAN

Restricted Trade

United States:
4th Best Outcome

Japan:
1st Best Outcome

United States:
3rd Best Outcome

Japan:
3rd Best Outcome

Source: International Credit Monitor.

In the real world, power affects trade relations. The continuing trade disputes between Japan and the United States demonstrate the effects an imbalance of power has on the dilemma of trade. Its position of power enables Japan to "impose its will" on the United States, the weaker nation. Therefore, Japan restricts trade, promises to open markets and breaks these promises, while the United States is unable to retaliate.

The situation is further aggravated by an unspoken realization that is more evident with each passing trade deficit figure. This realization is that the direct beneficiary of the economic dislocation the United States has suffered since 1982 has been Japan. In many respects Japan is now number one. The question of power—economic power, to be precise—comes into the picture. The reason Japan has been able to protect its own domestic market while enjoying unlimited access to the American consumer is that Japan can impose its will on the United States.

Consider the strained relations of recent years. Despite many promises by Japanese prime ministers, Japan continues to run enormous trade surpluses with the United States. In addition, America's current accounts spending is now financed to the tune of $100 billion a year by foreigners. Most of these foreigners are Japanese investors. Thus, Japan can exercise a great deal of leverage in the decisions it makes without fear of retaliation by the United States. When the Japanese continue to violate their signed agreements concerning commercial whaling, for example, there is nothing the United States can do to encourage compliance by the Japanese. They continue to do what is prudent for their economy, international accords notwithstanding, with complete immunity from retaliation. And when the United States imposes an embargo on Iranian oil in order to undermine Iran's ability to finance its war with Iraq, and its major allies around the world follow suit, the Japanese choose to disregard Washington's requests and they purchase almost 90 percent of Iran's oil exports.

These are two revealing, although much overlooked, situations that underscore the power relations between the United States and Japan. These areas of disagreement are manifestations of the ability of Japan to impose its will on others—in this case, the United States. It is not surprising, then, to find so much frustration against the Japanese in the United States. The clear loser in the current situation is America. The United States is denied the ability to compete in a highly sophisticated and affluent market. The consequences are felt in the United States through slower growth rates, slower employment gains, and reduced business activities. The Japanese enjoy what has been called an "unfair" advantage in the sense that they refuse to reciprocate on the terms of trade prevailing in the United States for Japanese producers.

Of equal concern, however, is that despite much discussion in Washington about imposing retaliatory restrictions against the Japanese—quotas, tariffs, or other forms of trade barriers—the real issue is being overlooked. The Japanese get away with imposing restrictions because they can. The United States is not in a position to retaliate without running the risk of duplicating the "beggar thy neighbor" policies of the 1930s that contributed to the severity of the Great Depression. Given the world stock market crash in October 1987, it would be inadvisable now to implement legislation that discourages trade. The federal and trade deficits, coupled with overwhelming levels of private, public, and corporate debt, impose narrow parameters in which policymakers can operate. The wrong legislation can undermine the already fragile economic base of the United States.

Talk of retaliation is not plausible for two reasons. First, the United States cannot afford to inadvertently create a recession, and second, all discussions of trade relations with the Japanese overlook the fundamental elements of the prisoner's dilemma. The reckless policies of the Reagan administration tripled the national debt, created a structural deficit economy, and sharply limited the options politicians have concerning fiscal and monetary policies. The absence of an international enforcement mechanism prevents two nations from abstaining from using economic power as the determining leverage over each other. The optimal outcome of the dilemma of trade will not prevail so long as the United States and Japan are not economic equals and so long as neither is willing to submit to arbitration by an international agency. The clear losers in all of this are, again, the consumers of both nations. The Japanese consumer is denied lower-priced, high-quality American goods and corporate America is limited in its operations in the lucrative Japanese market. The end result is that the average Japanese consumer pays exorbitant prices for such basic items as fresh produce while hundreds of American firms cannot compete in a market where they have a clear competitive advantage. This is the heavy price of a first best, least best dilemma of trade outcome.

Further complicating the assessments of the stands nations take concerning trade is the issue-specific nature of political rhetoric. In an age when politicians must limit the articulation of their positions to the ten seconds allocated by television broadcasts, it is not surprising to find the superficial statements tailor-made to the time constraints of modern media, resulting in contradictory, shallow, and inappropriate assessments of problems and implausible solutions. The protectionist ravings of some of the presidential candidates in 1988, for example, confirmed that the complex nature of trade, the challenges of dilemma-resolution considerations, and the importance of enforcement mechanisms in ensuring that an optimal outcome prevails were all somehow lost in the campaigns, debates, and public discussions.

For a nation facing the serious trade problems the United States is, it is imperative to understand the role of the prisoner's dilemma and the nature of trade relations as power relations in determining the characteristics of the global economy. There is no pretense made here that the prisoner's dilemma and the idea of trade as power can solve the trade problems of the United States. What is evident, however, is that thinking about the challenges the deterioration of the trade balance figures poses for the United States requires a thorough understanding of the nature of the problems. If corporate America is to regain its lost competitive advantage in the world economy and if the United States is to make sure that the power of free trade is harnessed for the benefit of all, then it is necessary to consider the insights possible through the above analysis of the trade problem.

In the chapters ahead we will examine trade theory, the role of the United States in the world economy, and how corporate America can take the initiative in achieving a sustainable competitive advantage in the global arena. The new administration in Washington must realize the importance to America's future of reversing the economic dislocation of the past decade. The 1990s will see an emphasis on strengthening trade agreements, expanding the role of GATT, promoting American exports abroad, and opening up lucrative markets throughout the world. Similar agendas are in order for corporate America. The executive who understands the nature of the dilemma of trade and how power relations determine trade relations, and can recognize the potential of the global opportunities available, will be in a position to implement sound strategies that can deliver a sustainable competitive advantage.

NOTES

1. Max Weber, *Max Weber on Law in Economy and Society* (Cambridge: Harvard University Press, 1954), p. 323.

2. U.S., Congress, House Committee on Energy and Commerce, 1985.

3. Richard McKenzie, "Textile Gripes Are Made of Whole Cloth," *Wall Street Journal*, April 8, 1988.

4. Ibid.

PART II

Resolving the Dilemma of Trade

REVERSING THE ECONOMIC DISLOCATION

The emergence of Western Europe and Japan as important economic powers, coupled with the massive transfer of economic power to a small group of oil-rich nations in the 1970s, has contributed to a shift in the world balance of power. With these new players on the world scene, the United States has been increasingly unable to "impose its will" on other nations. Thus, the resolution of the dilemma of trade has deteriorated from an American point of view. No longer able to enjoy the first best outcome, the United States now has to deal with other nations that have comparable levels of economic or political power. Indeed, the economic history of the United States in the postwar era is a distorted one. The preeminence of America in the world economy was due to the devastation wrought on the rest of the industrialized nations. Tom Peters, coauthor of *In Search of Excellence*, noted that "There were no competitors . . . we were living on an island and had no international competition."[1] While Western Europe and Japan began to rebuild their shattered economies, the United States, which emerged intact from the Second World War, enjoyed an undeniable competitive advantage if for no other reason than that corporate America stood alone. This absence of competition gave the United States a disproportionate amount of power. In the short to medium term, America would enjoy a competitive advantage that would erode as the economies of the war-weary nations began to recuperate. The United States had economic, military, and political power stemming from the absence of competition. This monopoly of sorts would last only until firms in Europe and Japan could regroup, grow, and enter the international market.

The disproportionate power the United States enjoyed, however, resulted in an interesting resolution of the dilemma of trade. Under the circumstances, the United States could restrict trade (made possible by the absence of international competition) while benefiting from unrestricted access to other nations. This was a first best outcome for the United States. Corporate America had unprecedented opportunities to export overseas and to penetrate market after market. The U.S. government was aware that if the nations of Western Europe and Japan were to recover there had to be an infusion of capital. From the viewpoint of this discussion the most important arrangement was the Marshall Plan. This program of economic aid was instrumental in helping foreign governments secure the necessary financing to ensure their economies were stable.

Most important, it prevented the emergence of a dependency relationship between the United States and its allies. It would have been reasonable to assume that the United States would grow from unrestricted trade, but the restrictions imposed on the trade of the other nation (in this case this was manifested as an absence of competition) would result in a dependence on the first nation. The United States would have run a trade surplus while the other nation would have incurred a deficit, and hence there would have been a net transfer to the United States. This is the kind of result that is seen when the United States restricts trade with small, underdeveloped nations while enjoying free access to those markets.

This did not occur in the case of Western Europe and Japan because of the Marshall Plan. While corporate America grew, enjoying surpluses and establishing itself in foreign markets— the ubiquitous Coca-Cola signs around the globe are testaments to American success—the assistance programs in place funneled enormous amounts of money back into these economies. In a way the U.S. government was giving billions of dollars to these economies that created a demand that could only be satisfied by American producers. The money the United States gave to the Europeans and Japanese found its way back into the coffers of corporate America. The trade surplus in manufactured goods was more than offset by the transfer of financial assistance to these nations. The net effect was a deficit. (The European and Japanese governments didn't spend every dollar on American imports. After all, they were busy helping domestic firms get on a firm footing and on public works projects to restore the cities destroyed by the war.) The United States incurred net deficits in order to transfer purchasing power to its allies. Had it not been for the Marshall Plan Europe and Japan would have become dependent on the United States and corporate America would have grown at a much slower rate due to the slower demand growth in the international market.

The situation that prevailed during the late 1940s and the 1950s was an unsustainable one. Corporate America could not continue to enjoy a first best, least best outcome indefinitely. The United States could not continue to transfer funds to her allies indefinitely. The American economy could not incur deficits indefinitely, nor could the dilemma of trade sustain a suboptimal outcome indefinitely. These facts became self-evident in the 1960s when Bretton Woods, the economic modus operandi of the world established after 1945, came under increasing pressure. This pressure, moreover, could be summarized in one word: competitors. The economic relief was working and the nations of Europe and Japan were coming into their own. As West Germany and Japan, especially, strengthened their economies the once-unchallenged firms of corporate America encountered competition on an international scale. The international economic order could not accommodate the emergence of so many players of great importance. This, coupled with other developments, such as the Vietnam War, exacerbated the situation. The world economy faced a series of exchange rate crises, trade disputes, and inflationary pressures. The crises culminated in the abandonment of the gold standard, floating exchange rates, and fundamental economic and trade disputes with our major trading partners.

To understand why the Bretton Woods system collapsed it is necessary to consider the dilemma of trade once more. Once the U.S. relief programs came to an end, the trade situation did not reflect the new circumstances. The United States still enjoyed access to these foreign markets, but it no longer interacted in these markets alone. The strengthening economies produced competitors. The suboptimal outcome the United States could impose on its trading partners could no longer be sustained once other nations increased their power. Had the situation remained unchanged, without the ameliorating effects of the Marshall Plan the nations of Western Europe and Japan would have become dependent on the United States. This is the inevitable outcome when two nations of unequal power trade in the absence of an enforcement mechanism. For the Europeans and for the Japanese it was simply unthinkable to become dependent on America. Their rapid recuperation from the devastations of the war and their historic political importance precluded allowing a suboptimal outcome to prevail for long.

The tensions between the United States and the industrialized world that characterized the 1960s were a manifestation of the ability of economic and political equals to deal with one another. The United Staes could not "impose" its will on nations such as France, West Germany, and Japan as it did on small nations of the world that were penalized, for example, in the Multi-Fibre Agreements. The outcome of the dilemma of trade had to be an equitable one that benefited all the trading partners. It was now that attention turned to the much-neglected GATT. This became a forum for negotiating the rules of trade that would ensure that full reciprocity prevailed. There were, however, a set of rules established to ensure that the special requirements of developing nations were taken into account.

Trade among equals, however, is a different matter where full reciprocity prevails. The history of GATT demonstrates a commitment to expanding trade on equal terms. As the dilemma of trade outcome has been renegotiated to reflect the needs of parties of relative equal power, corporate America has encountered a newly competitive business environment. "Is the United States losing its place as possessor of the world's strongest economy?" asked Leonard Silk of the *New York Times* in April 1988.[2] The dismal trade figures suggest little else (see

Figure 3.1). "Other nations are catching up," observed the authors of *American Business: A Two-Minute Warning*. "For the past
thirteen years 1973–86, Japan grew almost six times faster, France
and Germany over four times faster, and even England three
times faster than the United States. If those trends continue,
five nations—Canada, Germany, France, Norway and Bel-
gium—will pass the United States in productivity levels by the
turn of the century, and Japan will pass the United States level
in the year 2003," they concluded.[3]

The renegotiation of the dilemma of trade outcome has come
about by default. The emergence of formidable competitors on
the international scene occurred without much fanfare. The inability of corporate America to compete successfully against firms
of international stature has come as a rude awakening. Once
the unquestioned leader of the free world, today the United
States is besieged by competitors who are able to flourish—
even when their currencies have appreciated considerably against
the U.S. dollar. The econommic dislocation the United States
has endured is the mechanism by which the dilemma of trade
outcome has been renegotiated by the now-equal trading partners who have their own interests to pursue. The challenges
corporate America has not been able to meet demonstrate how
devastating complacency and lack of discipline can be for a nation. In the same manner that other nations have declined in
the past, such as the Netherlands and England, the United States
is now threatened by the stagnation of the past decade.

The danger for corporate America, however, is not the competition. Market forces and American innovation are capable of
identifying and correcting problems. The real danger lies in how
the situation is assessed. The most serious misconception in
current thinking is that the erosion of American preeminence
in the world economy can be corrected through the exchange
rates and with protectionist legislation. The increasing tide of
protectionist sentiment as the 1980s draw to a close bodes very
ill for the global economy. The failure to recognize the nature
of the beast will only serve to prolong the malaise afflicting the
American economy. Not unlike other nations that misread the
nature of their problems, such as England and Spain, and have
fallen into relative obscurity, the United States faces a chal-

Figure 3.1
U.S. Trade Deficit with Major Trading Partners

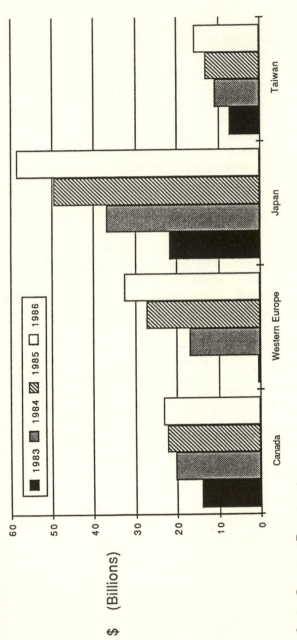

Source: Commerce Department.

lenge that requires immediate attention. As Paul Kennedy noted in *The Rise and Fall of the Great Powers*, "it simply has not been given to any one society to remain *permanently* ahead of all others, because that would imply a freezing of the differentiated pattern of growth rates, technological advance, and military developments which has existed since time immemorial . . . this reference does *not* imply that the United States is destined to shrink to . . . relative obscurity."[4]

On the contrary, Mr. Kennedy's arguments strengthen what this discussion has alluded to: the suboptimal outcome that the United States had the power to impose on its trading partners under Bretton Woods must now be replaced with an optimal outcome in which nations benefit equally. The mutual best possible world, which is a world of equals, must prevail. This, of course, requires adjustment, but that kind of adjustment has already been made through economic dislocation. The net transfer of economic and political power to other nations corresponds to their emergence as nations of equal importance (see Figure 3.2). The balance of power, which once tilted to the great benefit of the United States, has now leveled off. The most overt manifestation of the new balance of power can be seen in the inability of any single nation to "impose" its will on another.

This implies that equals must coordinate. Hence the increased cooperation among the industrialized nations. When the United States wishes to establish exchange rate policies, ministers from the Group of Five nations meet at the Plaza Hotel in New York City and announce a Plaza Accord in which a negotiated agreement is reached. This sharply contrasts with President Nixon's unilateral announcement to abandon the gold standard and let the dollar float. In the same manner that cooperation is required to ensure a satisfactory resolution to the dilemma of trade, equals must also cooperate in other spheres affecting trade. The need for cooperation is underscored by the frustration many have felt at GATT talks. It is counterproductive for all parties involved to have negotiation rounds drag on for years. It is as detrimental to have agreements disregarded or reduced to tests of will. When the United States uses its superior power over smaller nations in the area of textiles, the

Figure 3.2
Percentage Share of the U.S., European Community (10), Japan, EFTA, and Canada in Their Combined World Exports of Selected Commodity Categories

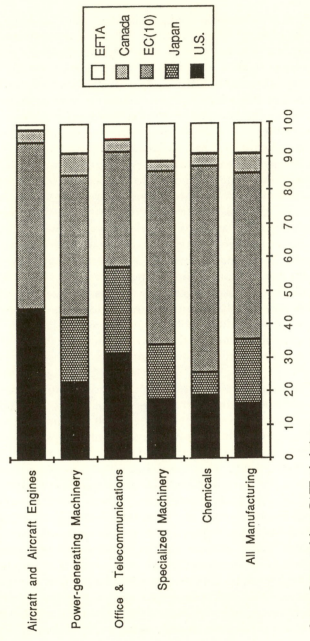

Source: Computed from GATT tabulations.

long-term interests of the global economy are undermined. When the Japanese violate the whaling quotas, under the transparent guise of scientific research, the long-term prospects of cooperation on other fronts are also undermined. Relations among equals are complex, interrelated, and require maturity if they are to be successful.

This is the reason the specter of protectionism is alarming. Not only does it undermine international cooperation, it reveals a lack of understanding and an element of fear on the part of American policymakers. Protectionism, after all, is the tactic of the weak and the scared. Efforts to impose restrictions on trade call for measures that would effectively destroy the first-difference provisions of GATT and invite retaliation by other nations. This is not becoming of a great power. This is exactly what England did with such tragic consequences. The more courageous position is to realize and to accept that a multipolar world in which there are several major economic powers is not an alarming proposition. An international community of relative equals is in the best interests of the United States. Only in such a community can the expenses incurred for services that benefit all—from military arrangements to scientific research—be shared on an equitable basis. If Japan and Western Europe bore a greater percentage of military and research expenses, vast resources would be freed up in the United States. These benefits aside, however, a community of equal powers is in the long-term interests of the United States.

The stagnation evident in Latin America and Africa, for example, is a direct result of a suboptimal outcome to the dilemma of trade. These nations, for the most part, are impoverished by trade because the greater power of other nations sentences them to a least best outcome. The gradual dependency—some would say bleeding—harms the long-term interests of the United States. When these nations have enormous foreign debts and experience stagnation, the prospects of American firms selling to the consumers of those nations are not bright. Corporate America would be best served if the nations of these continents were growing; what better markets? The shortsighted views of policymakers in Washington, however, undermine the prospects for these nations. If the policies advocated become law, the first-difference benefits afforded the poorer nations would be destroyed, leaving the international economy a bit more fragile. The interests of America are clearly in facilitating trade.

In order to do so, however, America must accept the inevitability that the world stage must now be shared with Japan and West Germany. Only then can the nation's attention focus on what is the only legitimate issue for America: how to achieve a sustainable competitive advantage in the international economy. Political rhetoric demanding protectionism, exorting retaliation, grumbling for a level playing field, and threatening punishment are all smoke-screen tactics that attempt to divert attention from the serious shortcomings in the national infrastructure that sabotage the chances of corporate America.

The truth of the matter is that the current situation in the United States must be addressed by both the public and corporate sectors. Corporate America must implement changes that will allow it to compete effectively in world markets. Government must in turn address the crisis in the educational system of this country that is turning out functional illiterates incapable of working in the private sector. The same kind of cooperation that sovereign states require to facilitate the smooth operation of the world economy must be mirrored on a domestic level. The primary responsibility for teaching individuals to read and write lies not with the private sector. By the same token, corporate America is deceiving itself if it blames its problems on the absence of protectionism. For far too long the attitude among policymakers and business executives alike has been not unlike that of the leaders in Orwell's *Animal Farm*: "All animals are equal, but some are more equal than others."[5] The United States may be the first among equals for now, but unless present trends are arrested, America will be replaced early in the next century by Japan.

The role of the United States in the world economy must be reassessed given today's economic realities. The United States no longer holds a position as the world economic leader, but rather as an economic equal. This requires a program to address the seven areas where corporate America falls short. The surprising ability of foreign firms to maintain a sustainable competitive advantage and win market share around the globe and in this country's domestic economy is a result of structural shortcomings in the way corporate America is presently organized. Despite the attention these shortcomings have received in the popular media and in the literature, progress has been slow. This could prove disasterous, for if America is to reverse the tide and reestablish its rightful place in the international arena, these issues must be addressed and, more important, resolved. American military superiority must be mirrored by a strong economic presence as well. The seven areas of concern for corporate America are economies of scale and scope, management skills, quality, customer orientation, export drive, improved education, and labor relations. In the following section each of these areas will be addressed and concrete proposals will be made. Government, too, has its work cut out. The need to abandon protectionist folly and implement sound national policies by the government will also be discussed in the sections that follow. A partnership between both sectors must be forged if success is to be secured.

U.S. LEGAL SYSTEM REFORMS

The problems encountered by the United States in the international markets stem in part from the organizational structure of the American economy. The corporate executive must realize that while there are many actions over which he has control and which he can implement within his firm, it is important to realize that the very structure of a society can promote or undermine the best-laid plans. The Japanese cultural trait of emphasizing the importance of education results in high school students who have mastered the basic skills necessary to contribute to society. In the United States, on the other hand, the low priority education is given results in an alarmingly high drop-out rate among high school students and those who graduate are prepared to flip hamburgers at McDonald's. Priorities reveal values and values are the driving force of any society. The values that have distinguished America, from the separation of powers in government to the premium placed on the rights of the individual, have their darker sides. While the United

States is unquestionably better off as a nation for its governmental structure and its value system, discussions of the secondary effects that inhibit an efficient operation in the business
world are rare. The secondary effects of how the government
is organized in the United States and how the ideas and rights
of an individual are conceptualized are known to everyone: resistance to cooperation and litigious proceedings.

As a result of the economic dislocation of the past decade the
nature of the secondary effects of the American identity have
become evident. Whereas in the past the United States dominated the world economy and it was one American firm competing with another firm—and presumably both firms shared
the traits consistent with the American identity—today corporate America is up against other firms that are not encumbered
by such traits. To understand this better, suppose two firms
are competing with each other and it just so happens the
spokesmen for both companies stutter. The handicaps cancel
each other out; since both spokesmen stutter, neither enjoys
an advantage over the other. Now imagine that another company whose spokesman does not stutter comes on the scene.
The new entrant now enjoys a competitive advantage.

The tendency to resort to litigation and the unwillingness to
cooperate are the handicaps of the American character that are
ever so evident in the newly competitive business environment
and that contribute to the difficulties being experienced by the
United States in the world economy. The firms of other nations, which are the products of other national characters, enjoy advantages over their American counterparts. The first cause
for concern is the litigious nature of American life. While other
nations have other mechanisms, such as arbitration, to resolve
disputes and consider lawsuits only as a last resort, the United
States is lawsuit happy; the courts are backlogged well into the
next decade. This propensity to sue is, ironically, a manifestation of the American ideal of defending one's rights and chal-
lenging the ability of others—government agencies as well as
private individuals—to "impose" their "will" on one. The tendency to use the courts as a first recourse is closely tied to the
notion of power struggles among different entities. The dilemma of trade has a direct counterpart in the domestic econ-

omy's nature. Another reason there are so many lawsuits is because there are so many lawyers. Consider the following: Japan has 14,000 practicing lawyers; the United States has 650,000 (see Figure 3.3). As the supply-siders are so fond of arguing, where there is a supply, there will surely be a demand. All these lawyers have to earn a living and they have no alternative but to "market" their services by encouraging litigation. The bright and talented men and women who could be contributing to strengthening the economy and producing something of value are instead arguing with each other over matters that could best be resolved by better contracts, or as a last resort, binding arbitration.

The disruptive effects of excessive litigation are well known. Consider the following points made by Michael O'Neill in an article which appeared in *The Wall Street Journal* on March 21, 1988. Mr. O'Neill laments that ever since the October 1987 crash of the stock market, the financial "experts" have been floundering, laying off brokers, and going into bankruptcy. The disarray in the markets has left much of the investing public without much of the information that is required to make informed investment decisions. Under such circumstances, "us amateurs" must take the initiative to solve America's economic problems, says O'Neill, "even if we think the M1 is a rifle."

For his part, Mr. O'Neill is prepared to contribute his very own export program, a "People Export Plan," or PEP for short. "In one grand sweep [the People Export Plan] could increase the efficiency of the economy, undermine foreign competitors and eventually wipe out our huge trade deficit." Not unlike other great minds, Mr. O'Neill recognizes that simplicity is essential to any successful program. The basis of his plan is that a society can increase its competitive power many times over simply by exporting its own economic defects to a rival. In this way, the United States could transfer its defects to other economic rivals, such as Japan.

In much the same way that an individual firm has to concentrate on its own competitive advantage, so must a nation. To that end Mr. O'Neill believes that the most serious defects in our economy are people. "Not the workers who improve the economy by making and doing, or even the drones who ac-

Figure 3.3
Number of Practicing Lawyers in the U.S. 1960–1995

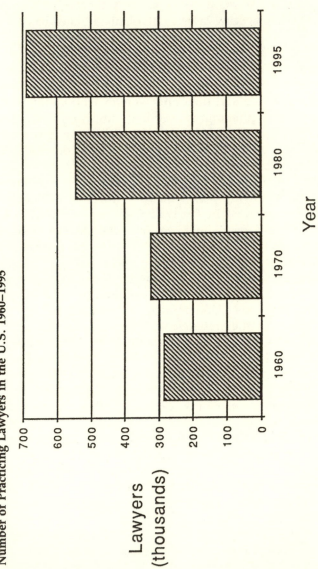

Source: U.S. Bureau of Labor Statistics, *Monthly Labor Review,* November 1985.

Note: Projected value for 1995.

complish nothing at all, like congressmen who can't even pass a budget," says O'Neill, "but the hot-tickets in our society. The yuppies—the lawyers, MBAs, management consultants and corporate raiders—everybody who makes millions tying knots in the coils of progress."

Of special concern to Mr. O'Neill is the lawsuit-happy mentality prevalent throughout the United States. The proliferation of suits on every level of society shifts vast amounts of valuable resources to inefficient sectors while depriving the more productive segments of the economy of needed skills. As Mr. O'Neill points out, although there are currently 650,000 practicing lawyers (one out of every 35 people in Washington is already a lawyer), the American Bar Foundation predicts that there will be more than a million by the mid-1990s. This helps explain the mess we're in. In addition, non-government law is a $52 billion industry. The Japanese meanwhile have only 14,000 practicing lawyers. This gives them a huge competitive advantage. Fortunately, however, it is one that O'Neill's PEP plan can overcome: export thousands of American lawyers to Tokyo! "By that one action we could clog Japan's economic arteries and clear many of our own."[6]

The humor underscores the frustration many in business feel at the mounting legal barriers to conducting business. The litigious nature of our society now threatens to overwhelm our ability to compete in the world economy. While we stutter in market after market, the Japanese and West Germans are ever so articulate.

The need to reform our litigious society will require ameliorating the American propensity to resist cooperation. Unlike other countries that are able to establish national priorities and secure the necessary cooperation among various sectors in order to achieve the desired goals, the United States is at a marked disadvantage. Attempts to address this issue, such as Sematech, are a welcome development. Only when there are the necessary infrastructures and networks and trust has been laid can the United States, as a nation, begin to work on the problems stemming from litigation. This cooperation is not exclusively the ability of firms in the same field to join forces, as is the effort in Sematech, but rather, it is the ability of firms to establish the most important of all cooperations—the relationship between the firm and its customer. Here is where the notion of cooperation comes into play. The firm and the customer are to be seen as partners in a joint venture: satisfying a customer's needs who, in turn, provides the firm with its livelihood. This is a fragile relationship that requires cooperation on both sides. The inability of American firms to grasp the essentials of this concept and transform it into a workable set of policies is one of the reasons the American consumer with his Almighty Dollar has turned to foreign producers. No one, after all, purchases a Japanese car with the expressed purpose of boosting Japan's GNP. The consumer purchases the automobile that delivers the best value. In other words, the consumer seeks out the most cooperative supplier who is sensitive to his needs. This lack of cooperation, coupled with the litigious nature of contemporary American society, contributes to the inability of American firms to compete on a global level. These two character flaws, if you will, are tightly interwoven into the fabric of the national character. To understand this better, consider the following study.

In the fall of 1988 when California voters went to the polls, there were several propositions on the ballot concerning the automobile insurance in the state. Since the early 1980s the automobile insurance rate premiums in California, as well as in many parts of the country, had been rising at rates considerably higher than would otherwise be justified by the Consumer Price Index. The insurance industry claimed these rate increases were necessary because of a "liability crisis" that resulted from record levels of lawsuits by Americans and record amounts of awards by juries. The result, in effect, was that insurance companies had to hike rates in order to cover the costs of doing business. But awards over $1 million dollars were rare and the number of suits was exaggerated. As the "crisis" continued, several states around the country began investigations. In early 1988 attorneys general around the country filed lawsuits against major insurance firms for price-fixing and violation of the antitrust laws. While state governments moved against the insurance firms, in California (where citizens are accustomed to the state's initiative process to pass laws, best exemplified by the "tax revolt" embodied in Proposition 13) several initiatives were placed on the November ballot that would mandate cuts in the auto insurance premiums of all California drivers.

This represented a major challenge to the insurance industry. The insurance industry faced a real crisis this time—but it wasn't the result of increased costs of doing business due to jury awards. The insurance industry not only faced lawsuits by several states around the country, but also the possibility that the lucrative California market would be lost. The insurance industry mobilized its vast resources and prepared to fight the "political crisis." The Insurance Industry Initiative Campaign Committee (IIICC) was established in an effort to "reshape voter opinion" and "convince" Californians that the "solution" to the "crisis" was the insurance industry's own no-fault initiative. This being the United States, while the IIICC began a $20 million "grassroots" campaign which, among other things, distributed petitions to thousands of California households and solicited $1 contributions from retired people living on pensions, the California Trial Lawyers Association (CTLA) filed suit against the IIICC.

The IIICC's response was quick: it supplied the industry's "best legal minds" at hearings in Sacramento while an alternative No-Fault Two petition, which omitted the clause found objectionable by the CTLA, began to circulate. "A strong grassroots network is the lifeblood of a successful initiative campaign," declared campaign manager, John Crosby, while checks for hundreds of thousands of dollars poured in from insurance companies all around the nation. Television and print ads, which mentioned the no-fault "solution" without bothering about minor details, such as informing the viewer or reader precisely what no-fault automobile insurance is and how it would affect the California driver, flooded the airways and filled the newspaper pages throughout the state. "More than 19,000 Californians have responded to the Campaign ads," declared the IIICC's campaign report. "Contributions ranging from $1 to $150 are pouring into our offices," the report went on to boast.[7]

The irony of it all, however, was that most of the Californians signing the petitions and sending contributions did so

without understanding what they were doing. "The vast majority of the mail we've opened is from individuals who think
we are *fighting* the insurance industry—they have no notion we
are the insurance industry," stated a campaign worker. "These
poor people send in sob stories about how high their premiums are, that they're retired folks living on fixed incomes, but
are nonetheless sending us the only dollar they have so we can
stick it to the insurance companies because sticking it to the
insurance industry would make their day," the IIICC staffer
said. Thus, the IIICC concluded that "California is a major
market for most insurance companies. The potential for change
in California traveling to other states is great. This compels us
to do everything we can to keep the California market free and
vigorous."[8]

Doing everything did not include resisting the compulsion to
deceive the California public. In the meantime, the CTLA successfully convinced the Third District Court of Appeals in Sacramento that the IIICC No-Fault Initiative violated the state's
Single Subject Rule. "It was a major blow," campaign manager
John Crosby announced. "No-Fault One initiative is not dead,"
Mr. Crosby announced, for the IIICC was—what else—immediately filing an appeal to the State Supreme Court.[9] The CTLA
stated that it was not about to let the IIICC manipulate unin-
formed voters and that it was opposed in principle to allowing
the insurance industry to "reform itself" by allowing the IIICC-
sponsored initiative to win in November. As an "insurance
policy" for the IIICC, moreover, No-Fault Two began to circulate around the state. "No-Fault Two is the same as No-Fault
One in every aspect," Marjorie Berte, the IIICC "grassroots"
coordinator maintained, "except that it deletes the section the
trial attorneys are claiming violates the [Single Subject] rule."[10]
And so it went on through the summer. The CTLA and the
IIICC were at each other's throats all summer long while Clin-
ton Reilly, IIICC's campaign consultants, continued its $7.8
million campaign to "reshape voter opinion" in California.

This black comedy of errors went on during the hot California summer. This situation, however, is serious for it underscores how the two American character flaws undermine the
ability of corporate America to compete in the world markets.

The most obvious objection to this kind of foolishness is that it is a waste of money, time, and human resources. Mr. Crosby must be a competent executive; otherwise he would not have been given the task of managing the $20 million IIICC campaign. It is therefore a waste of management talent to have him spend all his time on unproductive tasks. Major executives for Japanese and West German insurance companies are not involved in activities such as the IIICC. Ms. Berte is a fine administrator whose time is ill spent being the "grassroots" coordinator for a campaign bankrolled by the millions by the insurance industry. Her time would be better spent on other activities rather than trying to deceive a retired old man into giving his only disposable dollar to this cause.

These, however, are only the obvious objections to activities such as those of the IIICC. There are more fundamental issues that raise serious questions about the structure of corporate America in the late twentieth century. The litigious structure of American society is painfully evident. Governments sue private firms, private groups sue each other, and firms sue government bodies. The good-humored essay by Mr. O'Neill is not so funny anymore. The massive allocation of resources into initiating and defending legal proceedings deprives the economy of needed talent, time, and money while eroding the nation's competitiveness. Nations unencumbered by the expensive overhead required by litigation enjoy a strategic competitive advantage. The $52 billion litigation industry in the United States is a high cost to pay for a nation trying to recover lost ground in world markets. These resources would be better spent on more productive activities that encourage the kind of economic growth that strengthens the national economy and allows the United States to hold its own against foreign competitors in all sectors of the economy.

Needless litigation is a minor problem, however, when compared with the disturbing display of selfishness displayed by this particular industry. The implied raison d'être for business in other industrialized nations is that a firm is dependent on its customers for its continued existence. This assumption implies that there is a sense of cooperation and mutual respect; if firms are to thrive they must deal with their customers in an honest and fair manner. The crisis management techniques being perfected by the insurance industry, however, leave no doubt as to the absence of commitment from the industry to its customers. The problems of the insurance industry, whether in the form of lawsuits by the attorneys general of states across the nation or ratepayer revolts, demonstrate a betrayal of confidence.

The firm, or industry, that is capable of dealing in an honorable manner with its customer builds a foundation of trust that ensures success. The insurance industry characterized its crisis in California as a "political" crisis. This is very revealing. The insurance industry sees itself as operating in a political, and not economic, sphere. The Machiavellian implications of this assumption set the tone for all the industry's activities. The insurance industry sees itself as operating in the "legislative and regulatory arenas." Nowhere does it address how it can deliver a service to its customer at a competitive price. The emphasis seems to lie in how to manipulate the government in order to ensure that ratepayers—who are seen to exist solely to enrich the insurance companies—continue to pay premiums. This is the kind of arrogance that invites rebellion by customers.

The seven initiatives placed on the November 1988 ballot in California indicate that ratepayers have tired of being pawns in the legislative and regulatory arenas in which the insurance companies operate. The danger for corporate America is quite clear. The unwillingness of an industry to deal in an honest manner with its customers has now laid the groundwork for continued problems. Consumer advocates will endeavor to get government to regulate the industry more closely, attorneys will work to ensure that every move on the part of the industry is challenged in court, customers will demand that legislators address their concerns, and the industry is now in a defensive position in the courts, in the press, and with its customers. This is no time for major firms in any industry to be under indictment by several states across the country. This is no time to waste valuable resources on a campaign of deception. The long-term prospects for a rational resolution to the problems the industry faces are not well served by managers with no scruples who face indictments. The result of all this confusion is a great deal of turbulence. When this occurs, the industry has no choice but to funnel even more resources into legal defense and public relations in order to stave off, influence, or control factors which affect it.

The short-term requirements are enormous: $26 million, top management talent, and the "best legal minds" at the industry's disposal are being thrown into a campaign to fight the CTLA and "convince" the California voter that the answer to high automobile insurance premiums is no-fault. The long-term consequences are alarming: the insurance industry, through its own actions, has created a hostile atmosphere inviting sanctions and opening up the possibility that legislation will be passed that favors foreign firms. If, for example, Japanese and European insurers proposed a rate structure that reflected actual costs, limited liability provisions, and generally responded to the needs of consumers, the pressure legislators would feel to allow these foreign players into this domestic market could prove overwhelming. The groundwork for major gains being made by foreign insurers into the domestic automobile insurance business in the United States has been laid by U.S. insurers. When competent administrators such as Mr. Crosby and Ms. Berte waste their talents and time on activities such as IIICC, it does not bode well for their industry. When an industry has to spend millions and millions of dollars to defend itself against charges of violating antitrust laws, collusion, and price-fixing, the industry is harmed. "If we lose this year, we'll be back next year—provided we're not all indicted and jailed," admitted an IIICC staffer.[11] When voter opinion has to be reshaped, this reveals structural problems a television commercial cannot correct. The negative side of two American virtues has undermined an entire industry. While the insurance industry stutters as it seeks ways to defend itself and preserve a status quo that preys on the customer, the more reasonable and articulate words of foreign competitors are, like the sirens in the Odyssey, drawing more and more California drivers closer to them. Another industry stands to be undermined.

NOTES

1. Thomas J. Peters and Robert H. Waterman, Jr., *In Search of Excellence* (New York: Harper & Row, 1982), p. 32.

2. Leonard Silk, "Economic Scene," *New York Times*, April 1, 1988.

3. C. Jackson Grayson, Jr. and Carla O'Dell, *American Business: A Two-Minute Warning* (New York: The Free Press, 1988), p. 5.

4. Paul Kennedy, *The Rise and Fall of the Great Powers* (New York: Random House, 1987), p. 533.

5. George Orwell, *Animal Farm* (New York: New American Library, 1974), p. 123.

6. Michael O'Neill, *The Wall Street Journal*, March 21, 1988.

7. John Crosby, *The No-Fault Solution: Campaign Report*, vol. 1, no. 3, April 12, 1988, p. 2.

8. Telephone Interview, March 25, 1988.

9. Crosby, *The No-Fault Solution*, p. 1.

10. Marjorie Berte, *The No-Fault Solution: Campaign Report*, vol. 1, no. 3, April 20, 1988, p. 1.

11. Telephone Interview, March 25, 1988.

4

THE PROTECTIONIST THREAT

There are very real problems wrought by the litigious nature of American society. Not only does it reduce efficiency, it is distracting. While the best minds of the country should be concentrating on strengthening the economy and competing in the world arena, they are occupied with contrived lawsuits or engineering clever defenses. While thus distracted, insufficient attention is paid to the very real threat of protectionism. The mounting protectionist sentiment in the industrialized world poses a threat to the world economy. The ability of American firms to compete in the global arena is not served by legislation designed to limit the flow of trade. It is important to recognize that while protectionist legislation may offer relief to a specific domestic industry, the interests of corporate America are not served by the protectionist revival. As John Kenneth Galbraith noted with some irony: "A revival of protectionist sentiment and legislation in the older industrial countries having already occurred in the present, it will do so to even a greater degree in the future. Once protective tariffs were for infant industries; now they are for the old and putatively senile."[1] The sharp implication here is that the industrial countries have grown fat and lazy. If, as Mr. Galbraith suggests, creativity and innovation are found in more abundance among the developing nations of the world, then protectionism carries a cost that may be the industrial world's undoing: protecting uncompetitive in-

dustries only delays the day of reckoning when these industries must modernize.

Wilbur Newcomb, editor of the magazine, *American Textile
International* articulates a position in direct conflict with the textile industry's unending demands for protection from imports.
"Now is the time to buy and build," Mr. Newcomb writes.
"Sales and profits are high. . . . Consumers want to 'buy
American.' Let's give them the best products at the best prices.
But that can only be done with the latest technology. We cannot keep crying 'imports' to cover large pockets of inefficiency
remaining. Instead we need to make ours one of the most
modern manufacturing industries in the nation."[2] It is the for-
ward-thinking individuals who see the dangers that loom over
the horizon for those who would protect the "old and putatively senile" in corporate America. The challenges of the present economic dislocation require executives of action who are
willing to work hard to formulate the strategic thinking necessary to meet the demands of the newly competitive global
economy.

THE PROTECTIONIST ARGUMENT

These challenges have apparently been lost on policymakers.
The discussions of trade issues in Washington center on a series of retaliatory measures against offenders, real or imagined.
The calls for protectionism, moreover, fail to consider that the
inevitable dilemma of trade will not be satisfactorily resolved
unless there are negotiations with the major trading partners
to ensure that the optimal outcome prevails and that international bodies, such as GATT, are strengthened, and indeed, are
modified to function as enforcement mechanisms when disputes arise. The lack of a rational program capable of meeting
the challenges posed by the economic dislocation of the 1980s
does not bode well for the dawn of the next century. Upon
close inspection the arguments in favor of protectionism fall
short of the findings of empirical studies carried out in order
to analyze the effects of protectionist legislation on the economy and the business environment. Consider the following arguments used to support protectionism:

Income Preservation

Many advocates of protectionism argue that unless restrictions on trade are imposed to protect a specific industry there will be a loss of income among members of that group. The incomes of farmers are a likely target in industrialized countries. Whether it is farmers in the United States or in Japan, the agricultural sectors in these countries are organized and vocal about the need to limit imports of agricultural products, the urgency of price support, and the necessity for trade legislation that protects the incomes of farmers. The resulting complex support and import laws have given rise to an elaborate bureaucracy that oversees compliance with the protectionist laws favoring these groups. The problem, however, is that the consumers of the industrial countries that have adopted legislation designed to protect farm income bear the weight of the protectionism. Agricultural products in the industrialized countries are higher priced than they would otherwise be if the laws of supply and demand prevailed. Adding insult to injury, moreover, is that while the farmers and landowners may benefit from the protection, nothing is accomplished that cannot be done more efficiently with direct income transfers. Attempts to protect the incomes of certain groups in an economy can best be accomplished through direct income supports to the affected groups. Reliance on protectionism is ill advised for it creates unnecessary distortions in the economy, not the least of which is higher consumer prices.

Tit-for-Tat

The most common form of protectionism advocated in the late 1980s is the *threat* of protectionism. The United States and France have primarily relied on the threat of import controls in order to open up foreign markets. At first it may appear rather inconsequential to use a threat to achieve increased trade among nations, but there are risks with such strategies. If the other nation refuses to cooperate and calls the bluff—what then? If the threat is carried out, then both countries will be worse off, and if the threat is not implemented, then credibility is lost. A tit-for-tat strategy on trade can easily backfire when someone calls the bluff. In addition there is another, more insidious, consequence of a tit-for-tat strategy: it undermines the use of negotiations. Trade relations should be handled through diplomacy, negotiations, and agreements. When leaders of one nation issue implied threats to other nations, the whole system under which trade issues are resolved is weakened. The authority of GATT in such issues is eroded, it invites other governments to issue threats in turn, and the entire process of trade relations suffers. A tit-for-tat strategy to open markets is flawed. It works only occasionally, it can easily backfire, it invites retaliation, and it undermines the processes for conflict resolution. These are risks too great to be recklessly ignored. Trade should be encouraged and markets should be opened through negotiations and not through threats.

Level Playing Field

In the United States, especially, an argument that is gaining favor among proponents of protectionism is that it is necessary to ensure a "level playing field" on which to compete. A nation that is the target of criticism because of perceived unfair trading practices may or may not be guilty of the allegation made. To understand the reason for this it is important to review the accommodations made in GATT. To be sure, fair trade is the driving force behind GATT, but it is also important to recognize that there are differences among nations that must be taken into account. In part this stems from the unconscious recognition that the outcome of trade relations is a prisoner's dilemma in which power plays a role. This is why GATT distinguishes between *full* reciprocity and *first-difference* reciprocity. Full reciprocity, as the term implies, means there is mutual and full access to the markets of two nations. Most industrialized nations have full reciprocity with each other and most developing nations have full reciprocity among themselves as well. The notion is that when equals, whether a group of industrialized nations or a group of developing nations, trade among themselves, the same opportunities should exist among these trading states. The nature of their economic or political equality mandates an equal opportunity for producers of both nations to compete in each other's markets. This is the kind of reciprocity that constitutes a "level playing field" to most people. GATT, however, recognizes that what is appropriate among equals is unfair among nations of unequal power. First-difference reciprocity addresses the problems arising from trade among weak and powerful nations. Developing nations have lower standards of living than industrialized countries. Their economies are in the process of maturing. There are certain natural limitations on the ability of firms from such nations to compete one on one with firms of the developed world. For this reason GATT has a program of first-difference reciprocity under which trade relations between the developed and undeveloped nations operate to compensate for the weaker position of the developing nations. First-difference reciprocity is a controlled form of reciprocity at the margin under which trade is progressively liberalized as a nation develops. This is different from "unfair" trading practices, which are generally understood to mean nontariff barriers (NTB), direct or indirect subsidies to producers, dumping or other import restrictions. Those who call for protectionist measures, while disregarding the provisions made by GATT to protect the interests of all nations, threaten to undermine the progressive liberalization of trade that has occurred in the postwar era. Unfair trade relations among nations of equal stature *are* disruptive of the level playing field, but there are fundamental differences between the trade relations among nations of unequal power that cannot be overlooked without consequence.

Managing Adjustment

A common argument made in favor of import controls revolves around the need of modern states to manage structural change. If an industry is doomed by the emergence of more efficient foreign producers, then the least the affected industry can expect from its government is to manage adjustment in a way that eases the difficulties of structural changes. This is a valid argument. It would be an insensitive government that did not respond to the misfortunes of an affected group. The time necessary to retrain workers, modify the existing infrastructure for other activities, and facilitate transition to other economic activities may be great. There are, however, provisions in place to accommodate the requirements of structural change. If, for example, it is decided that bicycle seats are best made in Italy, and domestic producers are affected by the ability of Italian producers to wipe out the competition, then the producers for managing the necessary adjustments are spelled out in the Treaty of Rome. This treaty, a provision of GATT, spells out the steps allowed to establish a time frame for establishing import controls that ensure that structural change occurs in an orderly manner. It would be to no one's advantage for disruptive effects to prevail. This demonstrates that no extraordinary protectionist measures are required. Treaties in place today provide for the proper management of change. Additional protectionist measures undermine the effectiveness of present agreements.

Domestic Employment

When foreign firms are more efficient producers in a given industry, imports will rise. The sales of the domestic producers will level off and then begin to fall. The steel industry in the United States in the early 1980s underwent an important decline in sales as domestic consumers bought steel from foreign producers. Representatives from an affected industry are inclined to petition government officials for relief. If imports continue to rise, it is argued, there will be a further deterioration in the domestic producers' share of the market, which in turn will result in plant closings affecting the employment levels. Under these circumstances there is a great deal of pressure to impose quotas or voluntary export restraints on the foreign producers of steel. The purpose is to defend domestic employment levels in the affected industry. This works in the short term. There are, however, significant spillover effects that cancel out the short-lived benefits of protectionism. As the industry is insulated from competitors, there is little incentive to modernize or otherwise implement policies that will make domestic producers competitive again. In addition, consumers in

Figure 4.1
Exchange Rate Indexes of Japanese Yen Relative to U.S. Dollar
1970–1987

Source: Board of Governors of the Federal Reserve System, *Federal Reserve Bulletin.*

Note: February 1985 = 100.

this country are forced to purchase steel products that are more expensive than they would otherwise be if there were no restrictions on imports. It is not difficult to see that since steel is a component of so many other products, the costs of these products will also rise. The cycle of distortion begins and the final result is that, while jobs in one industry are protected, as many, if not more, are lost when the price of a basic material rises: All products containing steel are now more expensive, demand falls, sales fall, and employment in these industries is reduced. As the recovery in the steel industry since 1987 indicates, however, the income of workers in an industry cannot be protected by quotas or VERs (voluntary export restraints), but rather through competitive forces. The sharp devaluation of the dollar since 1985 resulted in a marked competitive advantage for domestic producers of steel (see Figure 4.1). The lower dollar lowered the cost of American steel when measured in foreign currencies, and at the same time, the price of foreign steel rose to compensate for the weaker dollar. The more favorable exchange rates, not protectionism, offered the American steel industry relief—and the incentive to use rising sales to modernize plants and become more aggressive in the international arena. The most efficient way to protect incomes is to remain competitive, and manageable exchange controls play an important role in an industry's ability to perform.

Protecting High Technology Industries

New high tech industries that are by their nature capital intensive and have long R&D time frames have been granted special protection from competition. The arguments in support of such legislation have been focused on two central themes. The most common argument is that the particular high tech industry is necessary for the national defense of the nation. Brazil's stance against allowing the import of computer, semiconductor, and software technologies is an example of the power of this argument. There is no advantage in demanding local actors to duplicate existing technology when it can be readily imported from abroad and modified to meet domestic requirements. The costs of reinventing the wheel are great and the nation that embarks on such a program does so at the risk of creating enormous distortions in its economy. This differs, quite naturally, from a high tech firm engaged in programs to advance mankind's knowledge; but then again, an industry that is on the threshold of the new is producing the kind of knowhow that cannot be imported from elsewhere; hence, there cannot be any protectionist legislation affecting new knowledge. The other argument in favor of protecting technology-dependent industries is a variation on the "infant industry" argument employed for other kinds of economic activities. Advocates of the infant industry argument maintain that the long development time and the high degree of capitalization required by a start-up high tech industry justify protection. If a nation's high tech firms cannot compete with the world's established firms, then it must be afforded legislative protection during its infant industry phase which is its learning period. The protection afforded is seen as temporary and would be phased out over a given time frame. The problem with this argument is that it implies a failure of the capital markets to function properly. The reason this is so is clear to see. To argue that infant industries require special protection because they must be weaned through the learning period before they can compete with established foreign firms is an admission that the capital markets are not capable of meeting the demands of the high tech industry. This is clearly not the case. If a nation's infant high tech industry cannot attract the necessary capital to finance its requirements during its initial phase, perhaps investors are not convinced that the proposed venture is worthy of investment. It is, after all, the responsibility of a firm to convince investors that it will deliver a competitive return on their investment, inclusive of compensation for risks incurred. The apparent inability of the start-up high tech firm to convince the capital markets that the proposed enterprise makes economic sense should be a warning to advocates of protectionism. While there may be information investors do not know, this is the exception to the rule. What is not exceptional, however, is for governments to embark on protectionist projects that result in white elephants, and this is of no use to anyone.

Strategic Industry Preservation

When an industry is regarded as a strategic industry, there is a great deal of pressure to protect it from foreign producers. Different nations have different priorities for what they consider of strategic importance for the well-being of the nation. National defense considerations often play a role in identifying strategic industries. Traditionally it has been the steel, aircraft, defense-related contractors, and agriculture sectors of a nation's economy that have been considered of strategic importance to the nation. Those who consider it unacceptable to allow domestic producers in these industries to decline argue in favor of import controls to insulate the domestic producers. There is nothing wrong with wanting to guarantee supplies of strategic commodities, but there are better alternatives for dealing with this problem. If any given good is considered of strategic national, economic, or defense interest, the most efficient mechanism for ensuring the survival of the domestic producers is through subsidies. There are, of course, administration problems with subsidies, and in many cases these have become excessive. Nevertheless, subsidies are superior to import controls for they function to lower the production costs of domestic producers without creating unintended distortions throughout the economy. Another alternative to a subsidy program is to stockpile strategic goods. If other countries are more efficient producers of steel, instead of subsidizing inefficient domestic producers, or worse yet resorting to import controls that create distortions, the most logical solution is to stockpile supplies of steel that could be used in times of emergency. Other commodities, such as foodstuffs, automobile parts, and computer microchips, can be stockpiled as well. When a nation maintains that the preservation of a strategic industry is in its national interest, subsidy programs, not protectionism, are the most efficient alternatives.

This overview of the major arguments in favor of protectionism reveals their inherent weaknesses. Import controls result in short-term benefits at best, but at the great risk of economic distortions. There is no national economic goal that cannot be achieved with managed trade, subsidies, income transfer programs, and stable exchange rates. The use of protectionism, moreover, is the tool of the weak within the industrialized world. The challenge is in resisting the temptation to impose import controls to satisfy narrow interests of the economy.

The above arguments in favor of protectionist measures clutter current economic and political literature. The rising protectionist sentiment in the United States is alarming, for increasing numbers of individuals are proposing measures that can, at best, offer short-term relief, and that all stand to impose the heavy burden of distortion on the economy.

THE COST OF THE PAST

Protectionism implies the preservation of the status quo. The problem, however, is that the world progresses. The pace at which information grows has continued to increase at a healthy clip. The resulting information adds to the body of knowledge our species can draw upon to use for our benefit. While ready applications of this knowledge may not be optimal—this is where wisdom comes in—the fact that new applications for technologies are a continuous process implies that the status quo must give way. Those who long for the preservation of the present fail to see that the future belongs to those who can make the most of the new.

Consider the following argument: America must impose restrictive legislation to protect the domestic steel and shoe industries. If the United States does not protect these industries, the proponents argue, the domestic industries will be overwhelmed by a flood of imports from such countries as Korea and Brazil. The result would be catastrophic, some argue, for it would result in the loss of thousands of American jobs and a new dependence on foreign sources for steel and shoes.

Now consider the arguments of then-governor Martin Van Buren to President Andrew Jackson in favor of "protecting" the canal transportation of the United States:

January 31, 1829

To: President Andrew Jackson

The canal system of this country is being threatened by the spread of a new form of transportation known as 'railroads.' The federal government must preserve the canals for the following reasons:
One. If canal boats are supplanted by 'railroads' serious unemployment will result. Captains, cooks, drivers, hostlers, repairmen and lock tenders will be left without means of livelihood, not to mention the numerous farmers now employed in growing hay for horses.
Two. Boat builders would suffer and towline, whip and harness makers would be left destitute.
Three. Canal boats are absolutely essential to the defense of the United States.
In the event of the expected trouble with England, the Erie Canal would be the only means by which we could ever move the supplies so vital to waging modern war.
For the above-mentioned reasons the government should create an Interstate Commerce Commission to protect the American people from the evils of 'railroads' and to preserve the canals for posterity.

As you may well know, Mr. President, 'railroad' carriages are pulled at the enormous speed of 15 miles per hour by 'engines' which, in addition to endangering life and limb of passengers, roar and snort their way through the countryside, setting fire to crops, scaring the livestock and frightening women and children. The Almighty certainly never intended that people should travel at such breakneck speed.

Martin Van Buren
Governor of New York[3]

The good governor, who later served as president, would have "protected" the United States from advances. The same is true today of other well-doers. Fortunately for this country it was spared Governor Van Buren's protection. The industry he wanted to preserve for future generations is an industry we have done very well without.

The question can now be asked of the well-intentioned plans of would-be protectionists: Does the future lie in the specific industry targeted for protection?

Too often the answer is no. While steel is an important part of an industrial economy, so is the cost of materials. The number of nations now producing vast amounts of steel has grown tremendously in this century. It would be almost inconceivable that in the event of a national emergency a ready supply of steel would be impossible to come by. If the Israelis are willing to sell arms to the Iranians in the name of mere profit, what ideological differences could there be to prevent some nation somewhere from supplying steel if the need arose? If the price of maintaining a domestic steel industry is, say, paying 20 percent more for steel, is it worth it?

Now the issue is placed in perspective: steel production was a national security issue in the nineteenth century, but the twenty-first century does not belong to the steel industry. Is the cost of paying higher prices for steel worth saving an industry that belongs to the past? Policymakers must decided if the nation is served by incurring an inefficiency that will constitute a distortion to all consumers and users of steel. The same arguments can be made against protecting the domestic shoe industries: If Brazil can beat us at a labor-intensive industry that requires little technological sophistication, what of it? Will

Table 4.1
Estimates of the Cost to U.S. Consumers of Protectionism in the Textile and Steel Industries

Sector	Year and Source	Cost ($ million)
Textile	1980/ Munger 1984	3,160[a]
Textile	1981/ Wolf 1982	2,000-4,000[b]
Steel	1980/ Consumers for World Trade 1984	7,250
Steel	1984/ Hickok 1985	2,000

Source: The World Bank, *World Development Report, 1987*.

a. Tariffs only
b. Quotas only

the shoe industry make or break the would-be superpower of the twenty-first century?

In addition to the arguments against protecting the past, there is the question of the actual cost of "saving" each job. The "costs" and "benefits" of saving a given job in a given industry are difficult to calculate. The costs must be calculated indirectly and the benefits are determined by complex estimates. The estimates must also ignore the costs of managerial inefficiency, opportunity costs of technology lags, and the effects of price changes on savings and investments. Furthermore, economists tend to be conservative in their calculation and as a result most estimates of the "costs" are too low while the "benefits" are somewhat exaggerated.

What is alarming, however, is that allowing for the conservative nature of the estimates (Table 4.1) the costs to consumers of protecting the textile and steel industries in the United States are great. The drag placed on the economy by these self-inflicted distortions is cause for alarm. Consumers are paying far more for textiles and steel than they would otherwise pay if the forces of supply and demand were not controlled.

Thus efforts to place tariffs or quotas on specific industries result in two developments: First, consumers pay for the costs of protectionism through higher prices. A disproportionate percentage of their income is spent on goods that have a lower free market value. Second, the economy as a whole must accommodate the distortions created by a conscious effort to preserve an industry of the past. The cumulative effect of such "protection" over the long run is the reduction of the standard of living for the domestic population and the proliferation of inefficent industries throughout the economy, weakening the economic and political position of the nation.

There are those who argue, however, that workers who would otherwise be displaced are served through protectionism. Steel and textile workers, for example, stand to lose their livelihoods if their industries are not protected. "The striking fact about protection to preserve jobs," the World Bank reported in 1987, "is that each job often ends up costing consumers more than the worker's salary."[4] The sad truth is evident in Figure 4.2. A nation that opts to protect inefficient industries incurs a significant loss on the endeavor.

For the steel industry in the United States, the result of VERs has been significant. In an effort to protect the steel industry when the dollar appreciated greatly in 1985, the United States persuaded other major steel producers to voluntarily limit their export of steel to the United States. As a result, prices rose sufficiently to make the domestic steel industry profitable. The purpose of this trade strategy was to raise prices far enough to preserve the domestic steel producers and save American jobs. As the figure shows, however, the cost of saving each job was enormous. VERs cost American consumers $114,000 per protected job. The average salary of a steel worker is considerably less than that sum. "For every dollar paid to steelworkers who would have lost their jobs," the World Bank reported in 1987, "consumers lost $35 and the U.S. economy as a whole lost $25."[5]

The question now becomes one of efficiency. If the steel industry is facing difficult times, it is important to examine the reasons that lie behind its troubles. There are only two possible reasons. First, other nations have faclities that are more technologically advanced and are thus able to benefit from the technological sophistication to produce economies of scale with which the United States cannot compete. If this is the case, then the

Figure 4.2
The Cost to Consumers of Preserving a Job in Selected Industries, 1983

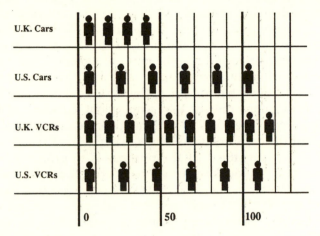

Source: The World Bank, *World Development Report 1987*, 152.

Each ![person icon] = the average industrial wage in the relevant country. Thus, for example, the cost of preserving the job of one British carworker is equivalent to the wages of four British industrial workers. Average industrial wages are based on the earnings of male manual workers in the United Kingdom and the earnings of nonsupervisory industrial workers in the United States.

most reasonable response would be to encourage modernization of capital stock within the steel industry. Second, other nations may enjoy a very competitive exchange rate that lowers their costs. The falling dollar has made the U.S. steel industry competitive with foreign firms. This is very revealing for it suggests that the troubles that plagued the steel industry were caused by Washington and not by lack of competitiveness within the steel industry. The overvalued dollar, a product of the high federal deficit and Federal Reserve policy, undermined the viability of the steel industry in the global marketplace. When policymakers turned their attention to the problems of the steelmakers, instead of addressing the overvalued dollar they enacted a body of protectionist legislation that not only cost consumers a great deal of money, but also created distortions that affected the entire economy.

The resurgence of the U.S. steel industry in late 1987 demonstrates that the revalued dollar lay at the root of the problems. This brings up a very important question: What is the real motive behind protecting an industry? Is it to perserve a domestic industry or protect the jobs of workers? If an industry is deemed of national importance and one that must be protected no matter what the price, there are certain choices to be made. First among these is the commitment to incur a cost over the long term. The costs of national defense, for example, are great, but the costs are deemed necessary if the Balance of Terror is to be maintained. If the purpose is to protect jobs and not maintain national security, there are other costs to consider. Is it better to spend $114,000 to keep a job that pays the worker $30,000? If the job was lost and the worker was paid his full salary, the economy would be better off to the tune of $84,000 per worker. Another option worthy of consideration is to pay the worker, say, 75 percent of his salary and spend the other 25 percent retraining him for another job. This maintains his standard of living while he is trained for another profession, while minimizing the distortions in the economy and allowing the laws of supply and demand to prevail in the marketplace.

This, of course, assumes that the malaise an industry faces requires any protectionism at all. In the case of the steel industry the solution lay in the exchange rate. Instead of addressing the problems caused by an overvalued currency, attempts at protecting jobs and an industry created a series of distortions that harmed the overall economy. The imposition of VERs on our trading partners limited trade, raised prices, and created a drag on the economy. The extra money consumers had to pay for steel—from cars to kitchen wares—could have been spent on other goods and services, strengthening those sectors of the economy.

As Martin Van Buren's letter suggests, he would have preferred an America in which the industrialization of the nation was slowed because of the restrictions placed on railroads, while a large expense was incurred subsidizing the canal system. Perhaps a large public works project in which captains would command empty ships up and down the canals, and cooks prepared meals for nonexistent passengers, drivers drove no one to and from the boats, boat builders built boats that were not needed, and whip and harness makers oversupplied their respective markets, all while railroads struggled to overcome legislated hurdles every step of the way in their goal of linking up the nation, is what Van Buren would have liked to have seen. The dangers of protecting industries are still present today. Paying $114,000 to keep a $30,000 job is not a bargain, and paying workers to produce a product no one wants or that can be purchased elsewhere at a lower price makes little sense.

TIT-FOR-TAT STRATEGIES

Tit-for-tat strategy consists of selected threats of sanctions in specific industries against equal trading partners exploiting an unfair advantage.

Consider the prisoner's dilemma once more. The most advantageous situation for one nation is to trade freely with another nation that faces restrictions. For Country B, the optimal situation is to allow no trade from Country A while it is permitted to trade with Country A. This was the situation between Japan and the United States regarding the construction business in Japan. While Japan (Country B) was given free access to bid, win, and participate in major construction projects for airport terminals, ports, bridges, and large public works in the United States, the United States (Country A) faced severe restrictions on how it could participate in the construction business in Japan. The resulting disequilibrium proved troubling.

One nation enjoyed the benefits of free trade without reciprocating. The tensions resulted in a long dispute that culminated in the threat of severe sanctions by the United States against Japan. It is clear from the prisoner's dilemma framework that a situation as inequitable as the one described cannot last long from Country A's point of view. If the nations in question are not economic, political, or military equals, as in this case, then the system of exploitation can be extended over a long period of time. When the nations in question are Japan and the United States, however, the friction created by this inequitable situation becomes a major issue.

The threatened sanctions enumerated by American policy-makers against Japanese concerns were real. If enacted, both nations would have been worse off. Had Country A retaliated against Country B, then trade would have been restricted by both nations, pushing them into a suboptimal outcome. The rational choice is negotiation and the threatened tit-for-tat strategy encouraged negotiation. In view of the fact that both nations are relative equals, then a negotiated settlement to ensure that the optimal outcome would prevail was almost inevitable. It is important to realize that while Japan (Country B) would "give in" on its present position, this was really nothing more than giving up an unfair advantage. Thus Japanese firms continue to participate actively in the American construction industry and the Japanese have now established the groundwork for American firms to compete in Japan.

The tit-for-tat strategy is appropriate among equals. When a trade dispute arises in which one nation clearly places restrictions on an industry where its own firms are not limited, a sound strategy is to threaten to establish parallel restrictions. Upon closer examination, the tit-for-tat resolution to unreciprocated terms of trade reveals its utility for addressing suboptimal prisoner's dilemma outcomes among trading partners of equal strength.

First, trade disputes arise when two trading partners of relative strength are in a suboptimal outcome. These partners must be of relative trading strengths, for a developing nation, limited by a weak economy, the absence of a sophisticated military, or with little political clout, must accept whatever terms are dictated by superior powers. Among nations of equal strength, however, the partner facing a disadvantageous situation is in a position to renegotiate terms.

Second, because relative equality affords the ability to renegotiate terms, the partner suffering from a suboptimal outcome can threaten tit-for-tat in an effort to turn the tables on its trading partner. The prosperity enjoyed by Country B comes at the expense of Country A. Unfortunately for Japan in this case, the United States is a formidable power that can limit the access of

Japanese firms to the very lucrative American market. This power, which many other nations lack, creates an equality of persuasion, if you will, to ensure that a process for resolving disputes is put in place. The ability to change the terms of trade for the country currently enjoying an unfair advantage is the mechanism that will ensure that both partners agree to sit down to a negotiating table.

Third, because the suffering nation is able to set in motion a round of negotiations to settle a dispute, it is evident there is a certain interdependence between both nations that makes co-operation—and trade—inevitable. When both nations realize that they would both be worse off if trade were interrupted, then this serves as an added impetus to cooperate and negotiate a reasonable settlement.

During the Tokyo-Washington dispute concerning the construction industry in Japan, retaliatory legislation had been prepared by Congress for the president's signature. The accord, reached days before the final deadline set by the Economic Policy Council, demonstrated, in the words of U.S. Trade Representative Clayton K. Yeutter that "the success of this effort means we can effectively manage bilateral disputes even when they are as politically contentious as this one."[6] The negotiated accord in effect established a level playing field for American firms competing for major public works projects in Japan. The same access and conditions Japanese firms enjoy in the American market would be reciprocated for American firms in the Japanese market. The negotiations made both nations reach the optimal outcome in the prisoner's dilemma faced. As Mr. Ichiro Ozawa, the deputy chief secretary of the Japanese cabinet said when the accord was announced, "We fully hope that U.S. companies will take advantage of the agreement by taking concrete action to seek construction business in Japan."[7]

When viewed in the context of the threatened tit-for-tat strategy employed by the United States, both parties realized the inevitability of a negotiated settlement. It cannot be denied that by allowing American firms access to their market the Japanese have ended the protectionism their domestic firms enjoyed. One has to examine what they managed to keep. In 1987, for example, Japanese construction contracts in the United States totaled over $3 billion. The total U.S. construction business in Japan, by contrast, was nonexistent in 1987. Thus Japan, by negotiating with an equal, managed to keep the handsome market share its firms enjoy in this country. Had the proposed legislation become law the retaliatory sanctions would have ended the advantages the Japanese enjoyed even though the U.S. position would not have improved at all. The most suboptimal outcome would have resulted.

Rational nations, motivated by self-interest if not belief in free trade, will almost certainly engage in a pragmatic approach to international trade disputes. The misguided policies of the past, such as the Smoot-Hawley Tariff Act (1930) which plunged the world into the Great Depression, would not so easily become law. In this instance the Japanese government not only negotiated an agreement that satisfied U.S. trade officials, but also deliberately disregarded the wishes of its domestic construction industry firms. It is so secret that in Japan the construction industry is a leading campaign contributor to many of the ruling Liberal Democratic Party's key members. The political pressure that had to be overcome in order to make the accord a reality is not to be underestimated. Then again, neither is a $3 billion market in the United States.

Thus while tit-for-tat will get a reluctant trading partner to the negotiating table and serve as an important impetus to reach an accord, it has no enforcement mechanism. The much-heralded announcement of the Tokyo-Washington accord on the construction industry, for example, had no enforcement mechanism. The success of the accord—and the ultimate success of American firms submitting bids for projects in Japan—will depend on the goodwill of the Japanese. If Tokyo does not implement the provisions established in the accord, there is little chance that an American firm will be awarded a bid. At present there are important public works projects in Japan for which American firms would do well to consider submitting bids. Major airport terminals for the Kansai, Haneda, and Narita airports are of significant value. In addition there is a great deal of interest in other major projects that are technology dependent. Most notable among these are the proposed "technoport" at Osaka and the Inland Sea intelligent building project.

The opportunities are there. What needs to be seen, however, is whether there is a commitment on the part of the Japanese to guarantee that the provisions agreed to in their accords will be implemented fully. The reluctance is but evident; Country B is asked to surrender its own optimal position, even though failure to do so would result in a significant deterioration. While it comes down to a question of either doing with less or doing with *a lot* less, no matter which choice is made there will be less. No matter where a politician is from, it is a formidable task to convince his constituents that an agreement that means less is the product of "successful" negotiations. It remains to be seen if the political will can be mustered to ensure that the established policies and procedures under which American firms can compete for public works contracts in Japan will result in important bids being awarded to U.S. companies. If it does, then the tit-for-tat strategy will have played an important role in ensuring that the optimal outcome for both parties is reached.

TOWARD AN INTERNATIONAL ORDER

The management problems encountered by contemporary nation-states are a direct result of the collapse of the Bretton Woods system. While few would argue that a return to that system would solve these problems, it must be remembered that Bretton Woods was dismantled only after the world's economies had outgrown the system. The principles on which Bretton Woods was built, however, are valid for our day. The principles of cooperation, monetary arrangements, and fiscal agreements are necessary if stability is to be restored to the world economy. The U.S. dollar began to rise in the early 1980s to unprecedented heights against the currencies of other industrialized nations. It peaked in February 1985 when, after much deliberation with other central banks, the major industrial nations, most notably the United States, Japan, West Germany, and the United Kingdom, began to intervene in the foreign exchange markets to check the dollar's rise. These operations were not completed without hesitation, confusion, and disagreements among treasury officials of the Group of Five nations.

Their reluctance to intervene in the markets is understandable, especially since the Reagan administration based its political and economic policies on the assumption that things work out for the best when the markets are left alone. The necessity, however, to lower the dollar in the hopes of reducing the U.S. trade deficits prevailed over ideological pretences. The dollar has declined considerably. While the trade deficit stubbornly lingers (see Figure 4.3), the weaker dollar has made many manufacturing industries, such as steel, competitive in the world markets. The prospects of the Rust Belt have greatly benefited from a weaker dollar.

There are, however, many industries that have yet to benefit. The fortunes of an individual industry, or firm for that matter, depend on the ability to recognize the opportunities exchange rates facilitate. Consider the long-term relationship between the exchange rate and trade balance. Most discussions of this topic focus on the role of a devaluation or an appreciation on the total balance of payments. After a devaluation, it is recognized, a nation's products are cheaper vis-à-vis those of foreign producers and foreign goods are now more expensive to the domestic consumer. The result is that foreigners begin to buy more from that nation while its domestic consumer substitutes domestic products for the more expensive imported ones. Exports rise, imports fall, and the trade balance is thus improved. When a nation's currency appreciates, the reverse occurs, thereby leading to a drop in exports, a rise in imports, and a deterioration of the net trade balance.

There are other considerations. The time period required to adjust the exchange rates among industrialized nations offers opportunities. Unlike devaluations in developing countries, where sharp devaluations occur overnight, most currency revaluations among industrialized nations are managed and target zones are established as guidelines. The result is a significant reduction in the level of uncertainty about the direction and magnitude of exchange rate realignments. Managed devaluations offer the corporate executive valuable opportunities. When the dollar hit record levels in the mid-1980s, many executives realized that in order to remain competitive significant amounts of production had to be transfered overseas. Produc-

Figure 4.3
Comparison Between the U.S. Dollar and Trade Deficit 1984-1987

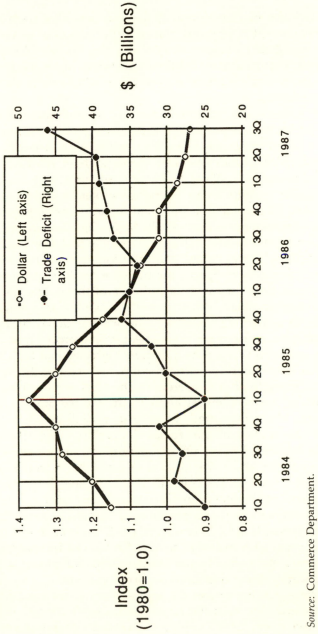

Source: Commerce Department.

Note: The index indicates the dollar's value as measured against the
currencies of 15 industrial countries.

tion facilities in Taiwan and Singapore benefited from American investment in physical plants and production, as did Mexico's *maquiladora* plants which string the border. Whether or not an executive articulated the opportunity an overvalued dollar offered may be doubtful, but the instincts were there and were followed.

The dollar's strength offered corporate America the opportunity to purchase prime real estate, production facilities, and secure investments overseas. The record-high strength of the American dollar made overseas investments in other currencies a relative bargain. While there was an important transfer of production facilities to an overseas market, this was not fully exploited. There was the potential for a greater integration of production resources that would hedge against currency fluctuations in the future. No one expected that the overvalued dollar could be maintained over the long term. This is why it was important to recognize the transitory nature of this opportunity and make the most of it then and there. The dollar has since been devalued. Whereas a dollar bought 250 yen in 1985 it bought a mere 125 by 1988. The weaker dollar means that investments overseas are now an expensive proposition. At the same time, the yen is now at record highs against the dollar.

What is noteworthy is that the Japanese realize the unprecedented strength of their currency. The high yen has resulted in a wave of Japanese investments in the United States. The uncertainty about the length of time there will be until the yen loses some of its value has fueled the rush to make investments in this country. The maturing Japanese economy requires integration on an international level to consolidate recent growth; the higher yen will accelerate the economic integration between the United States and Japan. The cost savings associated with a higher yen have encouraged many Japanese firms to switch production to American cities. It is ironic that some Japanese firms, such as Sony, have not ruled out the possibility of producing electronics in the United States for export to Japan. The cheaper dollar offsets transportation costs.

There is another reason the Japanese are so enthusiastic about making investments in the United States while the yen is strong: they realize that the high yen is a short-term phenomenon which cannot be sustained over a long period of time. "Stable long-term relationships among all currencies," Sam Kusumoto, president of Minolta Corporation, the American subsidiary of Minolta Camera Company, has said, "are vital to a healthy international business environment."[8] The exchange rate disparities, however, have opened a window of opportunity for the Japanese. Minolta itself is building a production facility in New York state to manufacture toner for photocopiers. Shawu Corporation is another Japanese firm entering the United States with record-breaking purchases of prime real estate properties in major American cities. These firms are joined by other Japanese concerns that are busy dotting the American landscape with Japanese facilities. The fact that many states are actively encouraging Japanese investments, throwing out the red carpet, and successfully wooing Japanese firms has served to hasten the activity. While corporate America did secure production facilities overseas, the wave of Japanese investments in the late 1980s was far more calculated, more organized, and more urgent in the attempt to maximize the value of the strong yen.

The difference between corporate America and corporate Japan, as seen in how each business community has reacted to its currency value, demonstrates again the Japanese commitment to the long-term scenario. Whereas corporate America moved production facilities overseas in order to improve next quarter's bottom line, the Japanese are thinking far ahead. The world is becoming a smaller place. The resulting interdependence requires firms that are truly multinational. As Mr. Kusumoto has said, "In the long run, increased Japanese investment and production [in the U.S.] and the corresponding reduction in imports from Japan will contribute to a more balanced, realistic bilateral relationship between the two countries."[9] This is one of the unspoken differences between the behavior of corporate America between 1982 and 1985 and corporate Japan between 1986 and 1990. The impetus of the strong yen on the Japanese executive has been to speed up plans to make the move to America. The strategy is sound, for it defuses a major point of contention between the two nations. If the Japanese are going to make so much money in the American market, then it is only fair that some of that money is reinvested in this country. The resulting improvement in the trade figures is a welcome bonus. In addition, the Japanese can claim that their presence in this country is positive: goods Americans want are produced domestically, employment rises, and the Japanese subsidiaries in the United States contribute to the nation's tax revenue base.

The economic dislocation the United States suffered has contributed to the politicalization of trade matters. The calls for protectionism reflect the anger and frustration of many in corporate America. It is interesting to see how the Japanese have recognized the need to diffuse political issues in a constructive manner. Instead of escalating the level of rhetoric by demanding that their politicians stand up to American protectionist threats and retaliate in kind, the business community of Japan has had the foresight to realize that if trade is to be preserved—and enhanced—then Japan will have to take measures that are not only good business decisions, but demonstrate a commitment to the markets that contribute so much to Japan's future. Japanese investment in the United States is a way of recycling profits back into the economy that is responsible for those profits. The long-term effect of all this investment will be to contribute to resolving the balance of payments crisis between the United States and Japan in a way that promotes and encourages an open trading system. As the century draws to a close, the differences—economic and political—between the investment strategies of corporate America and corporate Japan will be more evident.

THE LIMITS OF DEVALUATION

As the United States faced a soaring trade deficit with a soaring dollar, the pressures to lower the dollar mounted. The belief that a dollar devaluation would make imports more expensive in dollars while making American goods more competitive has a sound theoretical foundation. But there are limits to devaluation as a policy instrument. Consider developing nations that have been grossly mismanaged by incompetent technocrats. Mexico is a prime example. After the 1982 collapse of

Mexico's economy following its suspension of repayments, the Mexican government engaged in a program of making that nation more competitive through the use of devaluation. The result has been that the Mexican peso-U.S. dollar exchange rate has gone from 12.50 to 1.0 in 1982 to 2,400 to 1.0 by mid-1988 (see Figure 4.4). If devaluation alone was a sound policy for making a nation more competitive, then why is Mexico still in such a mess?

The United States would be shortsighted if it relied exclusively on a cheaper dollar to rectify the trade imbalance. As a currency falls in value, moreover, there are strong inflationary pressures. (Mexican inflation in 1987 was a troubling 179 percent.) The unexpected upturn in the rate of inflation in the beginning of the second quarter in 1988 reveals the underlying inflationary pressure that accompanies any steep devaluation.

There are, however, other dangers in devaluation. While the cheaper dollar makes American products more competitive, it also creates inflation in the form of higher prices for imported goods. Thus inflation is imported. On the domestic side, moreover, the rise in exports increases capacity use. "The nation's factories, mines and utilities operated at 82.9 percent of capacity . . . the highest operating level in more than eight years," reported the *New York Times* in the summer of 1988.[10] The inflationary pressures in the domestic economy rise with capacity use. Thus the potential for domestic inflation is increased. Unregulated or excessive devaluation contributes to both the importation and domestic production of inflation. A more insidious effect of devaluation is the lowering of the American standard of living. The rise in other currencies impoverishes domestic citizens; fewer can afford foreign goods, they are paid in a cheaper currency, and travel options are reduced. These basic and ominous ill effects of devaluation are one reason it so often fails. Consider the constant devaluations announced by many nations of the developing world: if devaluation were a solution, nations such as Israel and Bolivia would have devalued themselves into prosperity after all these years of countless devaluations. The fact that they have not and that they face severe economic difficulties underscores the limits of devalua-

Figure 4.4
Exchange Rates of Mexican Peso Relative to U.S. Dollar 1975–1987

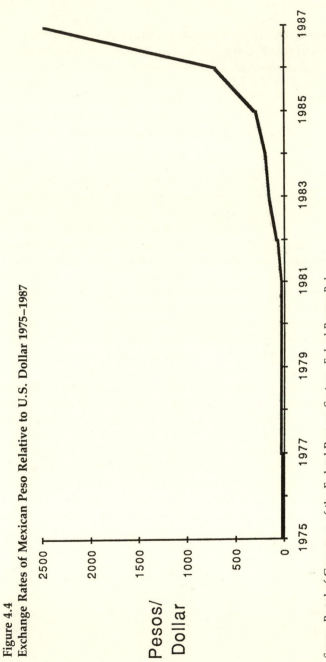

Pesos/
Dollar

Source: Board of Governors of the Federal Reserve System, *Federal Reserve Bulletin.*

tion as a policy tool. Indeed, devaluation is the strategy of the weak and its benefits, short-term in nature, do nothing for the structure of the economy.

NOTES

1. John Kenneth Galbraith, *Economics in Perspective* (Boston: Houghton Mifflin Company, 1987), pp. 294–295.

2. Wilbur Newcomb, *American Textile International*.

3. H. Jack Lang, *Letters in American History: Words to Remember* (New York: Harmony Books, 1982), p. 54.

4. The World Bank, *World Development Report, 1987* (New York: Oxford University Press, 1987), p. 152.

5. Ibid.

6. Clyde H. Farnsworth, "U.S. Contractors Win Role in Japan Projects," *New York Times*, March 30, 1988.

7. Ibid.

8. Sam Kusumoto, "Manager's Journal," *Wall Street Journal*, March 14, 1988.

9. Ibid.

10. *New York Times*, June 1988.

PART III

Management Strategies

CREATING A COMPETITIVE ADVANTAGE

TRADITIONAL COMPETITIVE STRATEGIES

Given the circumstances affecting the world's economies, a sustainable competitive advantage can be achieved through a strategic planning process that seeks to perfect one of the following areas of concentration:

Product Differentiation

The firm can concentrate its resources on the creation of a company in which the related business units concentrate on a group of highly differentiated products. The differentiation can be founded on various features. The most common mechanism for protecting physical aspects of product differentiation is patents that protect the trade secrets on a feature or group of features the firm's products have. Polaroid, for example, has a patent on the instant photography technology that prohibits competitors, such as Kodak or Fuji, from attempting to duplicate the technology. When a product's differentiation is based on an intangible asset, such as reputation or "quality," trade names are used to offer protection. Coca-Cola, for one, has a name that epitomizes the soft-drink industry. Regardless of actual preferences expressed in taste tests, the consumer chooses a soft drink not for taste, but for image. This has worked to the

advantage for Coca-Cola, for the majority of baby boomers as-
sociate the soft-drink vendor with childhood Americana mem-
ories and are loyal to the firm, the product, and the product's
aura. Thus the key to successful differentiation lies in buyer
identification. The consumer must perceive a certain value that
is intrinsic in the product and that no other competitor can offer. The successful company builds on one successful product
with a high degree of differentiation to create complementary
products. Both Polaroid and Coca-Cola have used successful
products to launch new ones. Polaroid offers several kinds of
cameras that use its instant photography technology to reach
various price niches in the consumer markets. Coca-Cola's Diet
Coke, likewise, uses the buyer identification to build a customer base of its own. The signal criteria used to create a sense
of continuity and reliability are identical: a series of iconic im-
ages, a distinct line of packaging or product design, and a solid
reputation. The success of one differentiated product estab-
lishes a foundation from which complementary products can
be launched; thus, a diversified corporation is possible.

Cost Advantage

The firm's business units can concentrate on reaching the
lowest delivered cost relative to the competitors' cost structures. This can be accomplished through various means. A firm
that concentrates on reducing costs by reducing the prices of
its inputs can employ four main techniques: bargaining power,
bulk purchases, the use of several suppliers, and transportation. The bargaining power of the firm with its suppliers or its
customers offers leverages that can reduce the costs of certain
inputs or sales to selected markets. At the same time, the firm
can make bulk purchases in order to benefit from volume discounts. This involves coordination among the firm's business
units to establish the horizontal linkages necessary for lines of
expertise to be of optimal benefit. The business units can pit
one supplier against the other in subtle ways so as to lower the
costs of inputs. The last area of external cost-cutting efforts
centers on transportation efficiencies. The firm that can develop an efficient transportation network can lower its costs

enough to achieve a competitive advantage. This, however, is not to say that cost reduction is limited to external functions. The greater areas for realizing a cost advantage are internal. Through a careful analysis of the internal value chain functions, whether production, operational, manufacturing, R&D, or distribution functions, the firm can sustain market leadership. In the wake of the market meltdown of October 1987 the investment community has had to cut costs. Charles Schwab & Company, a beleaguered firm in the postcrash market, has been forced to scale back its ambitious expansion program and lay off workers. Reduced trading activity by its shocked customers is one reason Charles Schwab announced that his firm would "reduce expenditures wherever possible." This retrenchment comes as no surprise. "Schwab & Company," declared investment banker Carlo Sensenhauser, "is a notoriously bloated company. This is due to its corporate history of undisciplined growth." For the San Francisco-based firm, moreover, the new austerity program has resulted in postponement of its plans to open thirty new offices here and abroad. The massive layoffs announced in 1988 revealed a failure to keep costs at bay through its program of implementing a company-wide hiring freeze. During the first half of 1988, there were several rounds of layoffs at Schwab offices nationwide, which came as a shock to employees who were assured that the hiring freeze and reassignment program announced shortly after the crash would be the most severe effects of the market meltdown. "The lack of management skill at Schwab's upper management level completely underestimated the consequences of the crash," noted Mr. Sensenhauser. "Their simplistic strategy was their own undoing and Schwab may very well be entering a period of retrenchment," he added. While other brokerage firms have been able to capitalize on their own strengths to consolidate their market positions and offer clients stability, Charles Schwab has failed to do so. "If Schwab's efforts to contain costs and streamline operations are managed in a successful manner, however, the crash may prove to be a blessing in disguise," he concluded, "though, from what I've seen so far, this remains to be seen."[1] The lack of capable managers at Schwab may make this goal an elusive one.

Market Focus

The firm can identify a particular target group and strive to meet the value chain needs of that market segment. The advantage in concentrating efforts on a few selected markets and customers lies in the specialization that is possible. When each business unit is working toward filling identified market niches, which, taken together, constitute a set of products that serve complementary needs of the customer, a certain dependence and buyer identification are fostered that lead to loyalty. Market focus, moreover, is an efficient strategy when each business unit is allowed to develop products that best fit its expertise. The firm, then, can develop within the parameters of a series of diversified related lines of business. The result is the emergence of the firm as the authority within the selected market niches. Rolls Royce, for example, epitomizes the ideal of a luxury automobile. It does not strive to be the fastest or give race car performance, but it is the most luxurious automobile made. The marketing strategy is aimed at the customer willing to settle for nothing but the most comfortable vehicle of outstanding workmanship. This does not limit the use of market focus to products with snob appeal. Federal Express, for one, has established a formidable reputation as a firm with impeccable customer service. In an age when telephones ring for a minute before a recording puts the customer on hold for another five minutes, Federal Express has an unequalled response time. The market-focus—firms that have little patience for waiting or excuses—has contributed to the stellar success of Federal Express. The pattern remains the same, however. Whether it is a car maker specializing in automobiles of uncompromising luxury targeted at a customer willing to pay a premium price or an overnight courier service offering unsurpassed customer service to demanding customers willing to pay a premium, the concentration on the needs of a particular customer and on creating a specialized product that is without equal allows for a thorough marketing program capable of achieving a sustained competitive advantage in the selected market niche.

GLOBAL STRATEGIES

There are circumstances under which no domestic firm has the resources necessary to compete against a foreign concern. The economies of scale required in many large manufacturing industries are enormous and represent prohibitive barriers of entry to many foreign private companies. Nations with fewer natural resources and smaller populations have difficulty achieving the economies of scale necessary to compete on an international level. If these nations were to rely exclusively on market forces to create domestic companies to compete in world markets, they would be at a competitive disadvantage. The result, then, has been that many foreign governments intervene in the marketplace in several industries—from airlines to oil companies to telecommunications firms—to create firms that are oftentimes nationalized or subsidized. Direct government intervention in the marketplace is the only efficient mechanism for many smaller nations to compete in a strategic manner with firms from the larger industrial economies. The existence of firms that respond to political as well as economic influences poses two major challenges for their American competitors.

The first consideration centers on the role governments play when they are the largest single shareholder in a company. The ability of the government to increase financing and its willingness to incur losses gives that foreign firm a competitive advantage over firms that do not enjoy access to government support or an understanding shareholder willing to incur losses in exchange for the promise of reaping benefits generations down the road. Many times, then, the question that impacts the competitive strategies of American firms is the role the nationalized or subsidized status of these firms plays during the penetration of markets or the bidding of projects. The long-term interests of the nation are manifested in the ability of the firm to price goods and services below costs. In the case of MITI (Ministry of International Trade and Industry) in Japan, for example, the partnership between government and industry works to advance the broad goals of the nation and the role each industry plays in the nation's development. The role of government as partner creates a set of priorities that differ from firms that are markedly less political. Through its power to give credit and approve plans, MITI exercises an important influence over the ability of Japanese firms to conduct business. Thus political considerations affect corporate strategies in Japan.

The terms of trade within an industry are changed when a major competitor is concerned not with market forces but with political ones. The attempts of many U.S. carriers, such as Pan Am, to introduce a more competitive fare structure among the European cities it serves have been thwarted by the adamant refusal of the West European nations to open up their markets—which are dominated by seminationalized domestic airlines—to the forces of the free market. With the exception of British Airways, which was privatized in the winter of 1987, all European airlines are government controlled, and there has been fierce political resistance to the notion of introducing competitive fare structures to flights within the European community. (The only other major private carrier, British Caledonian, was acquired by British Airways in the summer of 1987.) The ability of these airlines to charge relatively high fares on European routes allows them to subsidize overseas routes, competing with many airlines run by developing countries—most of which are former colonies. Air Afrique, for example, links France's former colonies to Paris.

The second consideration is that in many instances the nationalized or subsidized industry is viewed as a strategic industry necessary for the nation's security. In these cases the market served by the nationalized or subsidized firm is one the national government is not willing to allow foreign firms to enter. In the case of Aerolineas Argentinas, for example, the carrier functions not in accordance with the laws of supply and demand, but in accordance with the strategic needs of the nation. The purpose of Aerolineas Argentinas is to unite all the major urban areas in Argentina with air transportation regardless of the route's economic utility. Thus many firms are willing to incur losses in order to serve national goals. The goals range from supporting a national firm that is serving the domestic market, such as an airline, to providing a strategic service to the national population, such as supplying the nation's oil requirements, as is the case with British Petroleum.

The implications of these activities on global markets become evident when these firms are charged with strategic missions overseas. In many instances foreign firms operate overseas not to make a profit but rather to create jobs at home. The Japanese semiconductor industry, for example, is more concerned with increasing market share and the domestic political effects of a Japanese dominance in the microchip industry than it is with making a profit in its sales in the United States. Thus foreign firms are willing to earn lower returns in their U.S. operations—or even incur a loss—in return for higher employment at home. Foreign nationalized or subsidized firms that generate positive revenues from their international operations oftentimes serve national goals other than employment. As the debt problems of many developing nations become critical, the focus of these firms has been to capture hard currencies or improve the balance of payments. The criteria for continued aid and support from world financial institutions often rest on the ability of a nation to improve its economic picture. The ability to point to an improving balance of payments record helps offset failures, such as ineffective price stabilization efforts.

It becomes more difficult to compete with firms not concerned with short-term market forces. Indeed, American firms have to compete with many companies whose internal structures interfere with the natural outcome of supply and demand. The reason is that the focus of nationalized or subsidized firms is a long-term one. They are managed to operate with the future needs of their national economies in mind and can rely on short-term market intervention to subsidize future growth. In the case of Aerolineas Argentinas, for example, by incurring losses on unprofitable routes, it is hoped that the communities presently served at a loss to the carrier will develop at a faster pace than they would otherwise. Thus the future growth of these isolated communities is speeded up and in the long term the volume of business from the growing community will make the routes profitable. The national priority of these firms determines their behavior in the marketplace. The observed behavior in international markets is one of intervention. When foreign firms compete for markets with these firms, considerations other than market ones come into play. The

strategies of American firms must reflect the political considerations that affect the markets served, the prevailing price
structures, and the commodities offered by their competitors.
Airlines competing with Aerolineas Argentinas on international routes, for example, have to consider that airline's mandate to capture hard currencies. Thus, a carrier with a mandate
to capture U.S. dollars can be expected to economize on value
chain activities that can be supplied by Argentine companies
and offer marginal in-flight service. The competitive strategy
for an American competitor such as Pan Am lies in product
differentiation—excellent service, in-flight amenities such as
movies, and frequent flier mileage programs—and in targeting
price-inelastic market segments—business travelers as opposed
to tourists. Therefore, it comes as no surprise that on the New
York–Buenos Aires route, Pan Am targets the business traveler
who demands excellent service and is willing to pay a premium
for it, while Aerolinas Argentinas caters to tourists who fly coach
and are willing to endure some inconveniences in exchange for
a good bargain.

The behavior of most nationalized or subsidized firms reflects common patterns: long-term goals prevail over short-term
developments, market share is a higher priority than profits.
The lesson for American firms is clear. In a world characterized
by nations that rely on subsidizing or controlling large firms in
order to manifest national policies, the traditional myth of a
perfectly competitive marketplace governed by supply and demand rarely exists. The ability of salient firms to enter the U.S.
market or compete against U.S. firms for third-party markets
means that these firms are willing to accept lower returns. Their
priorities may lie in increasing employment at home, earning
hard currencies, improving balance of payments schedules, or
making a political statement. Under these conditions, the existence of nonmarket forces must be reflected in the strategic
planning process of the firm.

It is too easy to assume that fair competition becomes impossible under these circumstances, but this is not the case. The
existence of political-risk considerations has always existed and
will always exist. The difference is that during times of economic turbulence and technological revolutions that intensify

competition the role of these quasi-nationalized firms becomes more apparent. This is not to say that it is impossible to establish order and detect patterns of behavior whose impact can be quantified and incorporated into strategic planning. On the contrary, several discernable patterns of behavior emerge that result in predictable forces that affect the competitive environment in the global marketplace. The entry of nationalized and subsidized foreign firms into international markets results in increased competition, greater turbulence, higher levels of consolidation within the U.S. economy, and in an increase in joint ventures between American firms and foreign companies.

INCREASED COMPETITION

As the effects of the structural deficits and increased turbulence become more apparent, the increased competition in domestic and foreign markets will lead to lower profits. The national economies of the industrialized states are increasingly characterized by erratic and slower growth rates. As a consequence of these slower growth rates and stiffer competition, profit margins are reduced and there is increased pressure to trim operating costs. As the focus of competition turns to defending existing market shares, lower profitability can be expected, which will be exacerbated by the rise in the inflation rate. There are increasing pressures to monetize portions of the outstanding debt that cannot be ignored as a politically viable alternative. The persistence of structural deficits, increased foreign competition, falling domestic productivity, and lackluster growth will put a squeeze on profit margins.

The interaction of domestic macroeconomic forces and the differing priorities of other nations increases the level of uncertainty in the world arena. The increasing level of uncertainty requires greater flexibility in strategic plans and more widespread use of broad-based analysis tools capable of identifying threats and opportunities early on. In terms of market-area planning, greater weight must be given to determining the economic and political context existing in various industries while the utility of tools, such as the BCG matrix, diminishes. The importance of political risk-exposure rises, as does the importance of risk taking. The higher levels of turbulence mandate a higher willingness to make bold moves and put market leadership positions up for grabs. In the natural intercourse of market forces and competing national interests, the absence of international monetary arrangements and the continuing third world debt crisis necessitate the increased use of scenario planning and focused strategic planning.

THE INCREASE IN JOINT VENTURES

A natural outcome of intensified competition, higher levels of economic and political uncertainty, and the role of nonmarket factors is an increase in the tendency for consolidation within beleaguered industries. The rise in merger and acquisition activities in the United States (see Figure 5.1) underscores the subconscious need for achieving greater economies of scale. As if Adam Smith's invisible hand were the moving force, major consolidations in the banking, airline, and the semiconductor industries reveal the significant role economies of scale play in competing against formidable companies from abroad. The consolidation within these industries suggests that the need for the elmination of waste, the combining of R&D facilties, the extending of networks, and, at times, the radical changes in management-labor relationships are a requisite to the emergence of firms better able to compete on an international level.

Under these conditions, American firms will seek joint ventures with other U.S. firms or foreign firms to bid and to enter markets. Domestic competitors will enter into agreements to combine their expertise in seeking bid proposals or developing products. The emergence of joint ventures as an alternative to mergers, acquisitions, or hostile takeovers offers the flexibility of combining resources to compete for specific market segments or offer differentiated products to selected customers. The nature of these ventures is to give firms the ability to compete against the quasi-nationalized firms with a dominant presence in some strategic markets. The efforts of American Express to form a joint venture with the Soviet Union's Bank for Foreign Economic Affairs of the U.S.S.R. have been successful.

Figure 5.1
U.S. Merger and Acquisition Activity 1980–1986

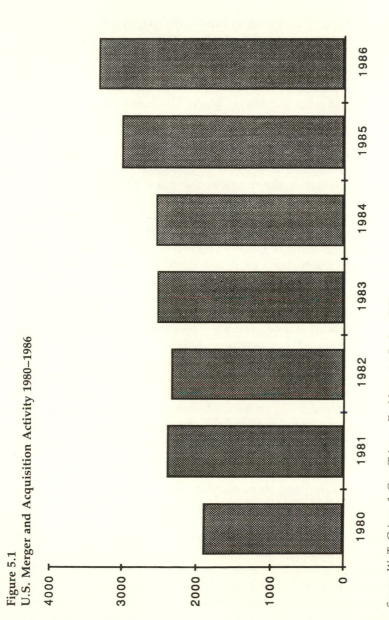

Source: W. T. Grimm & Co., Chicago, IL, *Mergerstat Review, 1986.*

The agreement, finalized in June 1988, grants the American Express Company permission to operate two cash-dispensing automated teller machines in the Soviet Union. These machines, which will dispense dollar traveler checks or Soviet rubles, are to be in operation by September 1988, and will be operated in conjunction with the Soviet bank. This, an outgrowth of Gorbachev's *glasnost*, is the first such joint venture with a Western firm. Here, then, is an example of the kind of cooperation possible with a foreign firm, cooperation that has positioned the American Express Company at a marked competitive advantage vis-à-vis its competitors in the travel-related services market.

The role of nonmarket forces in determining competitive advantages in global markets is increasing. The impact of quasi-nationalized firms is more apparent as markets face intensifying competition. The result is a world characterized by greater turbulence, slowing growth, reduced profits, increasing consolidations, and the proliferation of joint ventures. The cumulative effect of these forces emphasizes the heightened importance of incorporating context—economic and political—into the development of competitive strategies. The utility of using market-area planning in the formulation of corporate policies is more apparent as the degree of uncertainty in the world economy increases. The presence of nationalized and subsidized firms in the international arena undermines the strict adherence to free market principles and alters the terms of trade under which firms compete. It is under these conditions that the role of political and economic context takes on renewed importance. The policy lesson that stands out for the corporate executive is the significant role that scenario planning can play in helping firms establish strategies capable of delivering that competitive edge which too often proves to be so elusive.

Thus the lesson of these nonmarket forces is to reinforce the notion that strategic planning requires more than mere thought. It demands action. The proper role of the corporate strategist at the end of the twentieth century is not in compiling attractive binders full of information, but the formulation of strategies that identify one by one the steps, actions, and policies required to secure a sustainable competitive advantage. This is accomplished through differentiation, cost advantage, or market focus. The executive officer must be presented with a thorough set of strategies that offer the best course of action for each business unit, each good or service the firm markets, and for each kind of customer served.

The firm is only then in a position to evaluate each of the choices presented and decide upon a course of action. Once competitive strategies are formed, each business unit must endeavor to accomplish its mission. The overall strategy, moreover, must seek to establish a sustainable competitive advantage. This is possible only if the corporate business units reflect strength born out of their lines of expertise and shrewd positional strategies formulated from thorough and thoughtful market-area planning. The two prongs of this effort—internal cohesion and external relatedness—reinforce each other to achieve superior strategies relative to the competition.

PRODUCTIVITY

Whether or not the United States can emerge the stronger from the challenges it faces today will, in large part, depend on how it can gain power vis-à-vis other world players. The dilemma of trade can be more satisfactorily resolved from a position of strength. Only then can the optimal outcome prevail, as the parties involved recognize that the only reasonable solution to the dilemma is cooperation. The question now turns to how America can gain in power, that is, how it can improve its economic structure so as to negotiate from strength.

To understand how economic power is gained it is necessary to examine how it has been generated in the past. Robert M. Solow of the Massachusetts Institute of Technology, among others, has argued convincingly that in the American experience approximately 85 percent of economic growth, on a per capita basis, is a result of productivity gains or technological innovation. Historically, economic growth has been thought to be comprised of three basic inputs: capital, labor, and technological change. This label, as Ralph Landau argues, includes "other important elements: more efficient resource allocation and economies of scale as well as many social, educational and organizational factors that serve to improve the quality of labor and management."[2]

These points underscore what everyone suspects: productivity is more than the sum of the parts. Productivity is a measure of how a society is structured to compete in the modern world. The work of many economists in recent years has yielded some insights into how capital investment affects productivity rates (see Figure 5.2). France, for example, has an investment rate approximately twice that of the United States. Its productivity gains are also about double. When investment is made in R&D or in applying new technology, such as factory automation, capital interacts with technology to increase the growth rate over the long term.

The implications for this discussion are clear: An efficient way to increase the long-term growth rate of this country is to make a higher productivity growth rate a priority. The most efficient mechanism for this is to invest in new technology and know-how. An integral part of this requires not only doing what America has historically been able to do—implement new technology—but also investing in the quality of her human resources.

The need to invest in human resources is the more urgent, if for no other reason than the poor quality of public education. Many firms throughout corporate America are having difficulty finding workers who have the basic skills required to function in the business world. Indeed, the United States has continued a decade-old trend of producing an uneducated and unqualified work force. In recent years, the inadequacy of the American public education system has received a great deal of attention in the media, as well as among parents and employers.

This demise of America's ability to teach its children is no more apparent than in the high technology sector of U.S. industry. The body of statistics and studies compiled in recent years reveals that the number of scientists and engineers employed in the United States grew by 18 percent between 1964 and 1979, compared to 59 percent in Japan and 48 percent in West Germany. In addition, because high schools in Japan and Europe place greater emphasis on mathematical and scientific skills than do American high schools, workers in these coun-

Figure 5.2
Output per Hour as a Measure of Manufacturing Productivity in Selected Countries 1970–1985

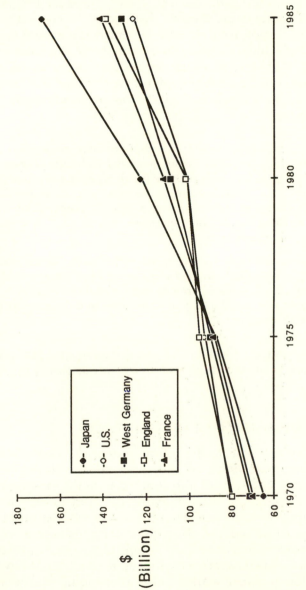

Source: U.S. Bureau of Labor Statistics, *Monthly Labor Review,* and *News Release USDL 87–237,* "International Comparisons of Manufacturing Productivity and Labor Cost Trends," June 15, 1987.

tries are better prepared and have a stronger background in technological issues than do their American counterparts.

These trends, coupled with the remarkable growth in the high-tech industries, have led to a shortage of scientists and engineers in the United States. In 1983, for example, the U.S. Department of Commerce issued a report titled *An Assessment of U.S. Competitiveness in High Technology Industries*, in which it stated that:

As a result of these trends, . . . the U.S. labor market was characterized by shortages of personnel in several high technology specialties. Most prominent . . . were those for all types of computer specialists. This reflected the burgeoning applications of computers and their related servicing industries throughout the economy. Similar situations were reported for electronic specialists and chemical, electrical and industrial engineers.

The increases in salary levels in the private sector, which resulted from a tight labor market, affected recruitment of instructors for U.S. engineering school faculties (currently there are 1,600 vacancies). . . . These increases also contributed to a sharp drop in the number of engineering Ph.D. candidates.[3]

A key factor critical to the development and the productive competitiveness of high technology industries is in short supply.

THE DELUSION OF TAILORED TRADE

While the path to the future is clear, it is not always easy. The corporate officer not only has to deal with the business of business, but he must also contend with the increased governmental nature of international trade. Add to this the various political ideologies and the economists who have political positions to defend and the picture becomes ever more cloudy. The modern executive must be able to navigate through murky political waters, keep his competitors at bay, and have insight into the dominant market forces affecting his business on a local, national, and international level. This is quite a task for even the most competent of managers.

World trade is a political issue. There is no escaping the fact that trade depends on the ability of government to facilitate trade. In this respect, then, corporate America cannot operate in the world economy divorced from political considerations. The nature of world trade makes business dependent on political systems to make trade possible and to liberalize commerce. Apart from this dependency there is another hidden danger that is often overlooked: discussions of trade inevitably are inseparable from policy considerations. For this reason it is not surprising to find the literature littered with arguments that are framed within the parameters of policy analysis pieces. This is unfortunate for it muddles an already complex issue. Given the mounting trade deficits, increasing competition from abroad, and the continuing loss of market shares to foreign competition, one can easily be seduced by simplistic and misleading ideas that promise a surefire cure or a quick fix to the current trade dilemma. The corporate executive would do well to be wary of such empty promises.

Consider recent arguments in favor of "tailored" trade. Proponents of tailored trade, such as Pat Choate and Juyne Linger, maintain that the economic dislocation the United States has suffered is a result of the fact that American policy has remained "locked in the past." American trade policy, they claim, is based on the idea that the United States is responsible for negotiating multilateral agreements to open markets and to facilitate free trade. The danger, however, is that there are currently five economic systems. These are: centrally planned, mixed, developing, plan-driven, and Anglo-American. Each economic system has different characteristics that require trade policies tailored to meet the demands of each model.

The argument sounds reasonable, except it's fiction. In an article by Mr. Choate and Ms. Linger in the *Harvard Business Review* entitled, "Tailored Trade: Dealing with the World as It Is," they spell out what the characteristics of the different economic systems are in the following manner:

In the rule-driven, market-oriented Anglo-American economic model, for instance, government sets the economic backdrop but takes few direct positions on which industries should exist, grow, or decline. In contrast, plan-driven economies like Japan's, and mixed economies, like Sweden's, skillfully blend the strength of government with the flexibility of the marketplace. Once decisions are made, government backs them with resources and, at strategic moments, with trade protection.

In free-market and plan-driven economies, private ownership of business and industry is the rule. The mixed economies, like France's, are based on a combination of state and private ownership, market and nonmarket decisions. Major industries are either owned by the state or tightly regulated. The major enterprises in the centrally planned economies, of course, are state owned.

The Anglo-American economies are process oriented; once rules are established, market processes dominate. The plan-driven economies are results oriented; business and government shape a national "vision" that often includes targeting certain industries like semiconductors or computers. To guide the economy toward desired results, governments of plan-driven economies will provide special financing, encourage joint research, and offer adjustment assistance like worker retraining. The mixed economies rely on a combination of market processes and government planning. The command economies are dominated by state planning.[4]

The problem with this description of "economic systems" is that they do not exist in fact. No economy is so clear cut. Thus, while the Anglo-American system is seen as one in which "government sets the economic backdrop . . . but takes few direct positions" is inconsistent with the many government programs to control events in the agricultural sector of the nation. The federal government subsidizes many farmers, creates distinct economic incentives on what is grown, purchases and stores surpluses, and maintains price supports for a number of products.

The Anglo-American system is also seen as one in which "private ownership of business and industry is the rule," but this does not describe the unusual relationship of government to basic utilities. Providers of all utility services in the United States—from telephone to electricity—are in fact in limbo between the private and public sectors. This limbo extends far beyond the role the government plays in setting prices charged customers, approving investments, and establishing guarantees on return, for it struggles with the very notion of ownership. In the state of California, for example, the Public Staff operates under the assumption that the risks of business are incurred by *both* the individual shareholder in a utility and the ratepayer who uses the product. A nation that is struggling to define limits and draw lines on fundamental issues such as these cannot be classified as black and white as Mr. Choate and Ms. Linger propose to do.

The Anglo-American economies, they argue, "are process oriented; once rules are established, market processes dominate." This clearly is not the case in the defense industry. The relationship that exists between the Pentagon and its suppliers taxes the very definition of a free enterprise system. The Pentagon dictates terms, requires that supplier personnel meet its criteria (including security clearances for some positions), prohibits suppliers from conducting business with others unless it is so approved by the Pentagon, sets prices, timetables, and controls over what is produced, under which conditions, and by whom. The nature of an oligopoly is very similar to the distinctions drawn by Mr. Choate and Ms. Linger when they define "centrally planned," "mixed," and "developing" economic systems.

Clearly, when one considers the portion of the American GNP comprised of the agricultural, utilities, and defense industry sectors, one is talking about a significant amount. In fact, just over half of the U.S. GNP defies the characteristics of the "Anglo-American" economic system. What then? It is clearly not reasonable for a nation to base its trading policies on ideas that are so incomplete. The essence of tailored trade is that it would allow "American representatives to match the negotiations to the economic system with which we were negotiating. For example, talks would draw free-trade arrangements with free-trade economies, managed-trade agreements with managed-trade economies."[5] This is a mere variation on the arguments calling for "fair" trade instead of free trade.

The criticism that applies to the fair trade argument applies to the tailored trade argument: it undermines the authority of GATT and attempts to consider issues for which provisions presently exist under the Treaty of Rome. If the problems we are experiencing in managing the global economy occur when these agreements are already in place, there is no guarantee that adding tailored trade legislation would make things any better. Of greater concern, however, is that arguments calling for tailored trade, a tit-for-tat scenario, are disguised protectionism. Tailored trade would establish one set of rules under which open, industrialized economies would operate while establishing a different set of rules for the developing world. This runs counter to the aim of GATT: that of helping to integrate all economies into the world trade system. The practical effects of tailored trade would be to erect import controls on trade with the developing world. This would invite retaliation.

The arguments in favor of tailored trade seem benign at first, but each unilateral decision to impose import restrictions or establish parameters within which agreements are negotiated undermines an open trading system. The tailored trade proposed is a delusion for the United States. Once nations are classified into "economic systems" and trade representatives agree to negotiate for free trade with some and for managed trade with others, there are long-term problems. First, the rules under which GATT operates are weakened; the mechanism in place to facilitate trade between powerful and powerless nations becomes less credible if it is ignored. Second, tailored trade justifies protectionist measures, such as textile import controls, automobile quotas, and restrictions on microchips. Those who favor tailored trade are providing the theoretical foundation for politicians to propose a piece of protectionist legislation that merely protects special interest groups and does nothing to promote fair trade. In such an environment the liberalization of trade suffers and there is an impetus for other countries to retaliate.

The delusion of tailored trade is self-evident when the assumptions are penetrated. The idea of tailored trade is a delusion because it assumes that nations who do not cooperate do so of their own volition. This is clearly not the case. The dilemma of trade is an intricate power struggle. As the prisoner's dilemma demonstrated, the stalemate between the United States and Brazil is inevitable given the circumstances of the world as it is. Mr. Choate and Ms. Linger argue that "the momentum created by [tailored trade] represents a formidable incentive for

uncooperative nations to end their delaying tactics and participate in trade talks."[6] This may be true in some instances, but
as the U.S.-Brazil deadlock demonstrates "delaying tactics" are,
in many cases, inevitable. Tailored trade ignores the very real
dilemma of trade relations among sovereign states who have
different degrees of power and no enforcement mechanism to
arbitrate disputes. As for the notion that tailored trade would
strive "to expand trade," it remains unclear how trade can be
expanded using such a convoluted strategy. Considering the
provision of first-difference and full reciprocity already existing
in GATT, one would have to question the effectiveness of beginning from scratch. The issues raised by advocates of tailored
trade can be effectively addressed through the Treaty of Rome
and the first-difference and full reciprocity provisions of GATT.
When there is already an international organization to which
most of the world's nations belong, it is of questionable merit
to disregard this body and embark on a course that requires, at
minimum, five trade strategies. If the world's governments
cannot manage to operate under GATT, which has only *two*
trade classifications, it is doubtful that the world's governments could manage under tailored trade, which has *five* trade
classifications. The United States stands to make an already
complicated issue even more complex. The United States cannot afford to unilaterally reduce GATT to a "second-tier forum."
It would be more prudent to push for giving GATT enforcement powers in order to ensure that states are in compliance
with GATT rulings. The grouping of nations into artificial classifications that, as we have seen, have little basis in fact serves
no purpose. If GATT is ineffectual, it is because it is not being
used as thoroughly as it should be. There are two strong reasons for strengthening GATT: the Soviet Union and the People's Republic of China both want to become members. The
most efficient course of action would be to build on the existing
trading system and to use it fully rather than to pursue some
ill-conceived notions of a world that does not exist.

In addition, when considered from a philosophical perspective, tailored trade denies the validity of Adam Smith's invisible hand. True proponents of free trade acknowledge that, as
Smith argued, each individual, when pursuing what is in his

best interest, serves the collective good. What applies to a community of individuals also applies to a group of sovereign states. Each state, trying to pursue what is in its own best interest, strengthens the community. Adam Smith's invisible hand works for both individuals and states. To claim otherwise is to undermine the foundation on which free trade, which has benefited the world economy to such a great extent, is based. The idea of tailored trade is clearly a delusion that, if implemented, would undermine confidence in free trade, erode respect for international trade organizations, ignore the real dilemma of trade that every state faces, and lead to a destructive escalation of retaliation that would benefit no one.

NOTES

1. Telephone interview, May 10, 1988.

2. Ralph Landau, "U.S. Economic Growth," *Scientific American*, vol. 258, no. 6 (June 1988), p. 46.

3. U.S. Department of Commerce, *An Assessment of U.S. Competitiveness in High Technology Industries*, February 1983, p. 25.

4. Pat Choate and Juyne Linger, "Tailored Trade: Dealing with the World as It Is," *Harvard Business Review*, January-February 1988, pp. 86–93.

5. Ibid.

6. Ibid.

FOCUSING ON STRENGTHS

The implicit argument made above to build on the existing system of world trade and to strengthen that system has its parallel in corporate America: build on inherent strengths. The price of holding on to a nostalgic past is great; nations that cannot look to their future may have none. England has paid a dear price for the vanities of clinging ever so desperately to the idea of the Empire; Mexico's future is hostage to its tragic past. The sentimentality that evokes arguments similar to those of Van Buren's is misguided. The future lies in focusing on a nation's strength. Let the fortunes of the steel industry lie in its own competitiveness; the obligations of government should focus on maintaining fiscal and monetary policies that stabilize the exchange rates. The steel industry's management should thrive or perish based on its management skills. Let Brazil make all the shoes it wants. If it can produce shoes of superior quality at lower prices, then both nations will be better off.

The strength of the United States lies in technology and innovation. These are the industries of the future. In the broader context of the national economy the United States enjoys a tremendous competitive advantage in the field of knowledge. The Japanese may be better at imitation, but no nation is better at innovation. The Koreans and Brazilians may produce steel and shoes cheaper, but if their high-tech factories operate on the advanced microchips and sophisticated computer programs produced by U.S. engineers, they will be dependent on our knowledge (see Figure 6.1).

When two countries are dependent on each other, there is an equality established that results in a negotiated best outcome for both. Recall the prisoner's dilemma. The nation that is able to create an undeniable interdependence with its trading partners will always have negotiation as an option. Instead of fostering a negative paternalism, the United States should focus on its strengths and on innovative ways of restructuring how the high tech industry operates in order to promote the necessary activities that will guarantee an enduring competitive advantage in terms of high tech innovation.

To this end Sematech is a step in the right direction. The advantage Japan enjoys through the Ministry of International Trade and Industry (MITI) enables private business to implement long-term programs. The emphasis on short-term performance in the United States, in contrast, undermines the ability of American firms to focus on their strengths within a long-term time frame. The Japanese microchip industry demonstrates that there is a significant competitive advantage to be had by being committed to the long term. The support of MITI allowed Japanese competitors to pour millions of dollars into the construction of state-of-the-art facilities at favorable financing rates in order to achieve a sustainable cost advantage over American firms. The arrangement fostered by MITI permitted private Japanese firms to allocate vast amounts of resources to this capital-intensive and long-term investment without having to worry about short-term profits and pleasing shareholders. As Edwin O. Reischauer observed, "MITI saw to it that the most advanced new technology was acquired on the most favorable terms by those best able to use it, but at the same time it ensured that there would be two or more rival private companies in each field to provide the efficiency that competition alone could produce. In this way Japan had the advantage of careful government planning for its overall economy—that is, the macroeconomy—while maintaining efficiency through vigorous competition among large rival firms in the microeconomy."[1] The success of Japan in the microchip industry speaks

Figure 6.1
Relative Resource Endowments of Selected Countries as a Percentage of World Total, 1980

Source: J. Mutti and P. Morici, *Changing Pattern of U.S. Industrial Activity and Comparative Advantage*, National Planning Association, NSF, Science Indicators, Washington, D.C.

Note: Computed from a set of 34 countries, which in 1980 accounted for over 85 percent of total gross domestic product among market economies.

for itself: in 1987 the Japanese held 85 percent of the world microchip market.

Their success was so impressive that it was viewed as a national security threat by the United States. The Defense Science Board, an advisory committee to the U.S. secretary of defense, warned of a dangerous structural weakness in the domestic chip-maker industry. The Semiconductor Industry Association was equally alarmed at the turn of events—in 1986 the industry lost $1 billion. The domestic chip-maker industry could not compete against an economy structured around a government agency as it is in Japan. The central role of MITI in the economic life of Japan brings up a major issue for American corporations on how to structure an industry to be competitive in nations with dissimilar economies.

The ideal of a free market is just that, an ideal. There are few, if any, markets free of distortions of some kind. As Edwin Reischauer pointed out, MITI has served Japan very well. The ability of the United States to respond effectively will depend to a large degree on the success of Sematech. The Semiconductor Industry Association proposed a consortium of chip makers and government agencies to respond to the Japanese challenge. The road to establishing Sematech has been a difficult one. As first proposed by Charles E. Sporck, president and chief executive of National Semiconductor Corporation, Sematech was considered by firms such as IBM to be nothing but an elaborate government bailout program for the troubled industry. The strategic mission, however, has shifted.

Sematech is now envisioned as a partnership between the private and public sectors in the United States. The proposed budget for Sematech is $1.5 billion over six years, half coming from the government and the remainder from the private-sector members of the consortium. The economies of scale possible through the pooling of resources is necessary because, in the words of National Semiconductor's Charles Sporck, "the only way [to meet the Japanese challenge] is to do things so that each of our companies doesn't have to replicate the same development process."[2] The success of Sematech is crucial to the United States. Without a comprehensive program to focus on this nation's strengths, regaining lost world market shares will be a difficult, if not impossible, task.

There are, however, major cultural obstacles that Sematech must first overcome. As John Kenneth Galbraith has observed, "In Japan the state is indeed, as Marx held, the executive committee of the capitalist class; this is normal and natural. . . . The result is an accepted cooperation between industry and government—public investment, planning and support to technological innovation—that is unthinkable, to the extent that it is not thought subversive, in the American and British tradition."[3] Perhaps. Then again, perhaps not. It is not that radical a notion to suggest that just as certain industries are regulated by the state—the regional baby bells, for example,—the same cooperation could be extended to other industries of national importance. John Kenneth Galbraith correctly observes that the cultural and economic histories of the United States differ from those of Japan. There may be a middle road, one in which there is a series of incentives, guidance, and cooperation from the government to support strategic industries of national importance. Sematech may very well pioneer this kind of cooperation between the private and public sectors.

The strategic mission of Sematech in the overall trade strategy of this nation is without precedent. The involvement—and role as executive committee—of the Defense Department in Sematech may very well serve as a prototype for other endeavors. Whether Americans can strike a balance between the private sector and government that enables the venture to achieve its task remains to be seen, but there are important characteristics of how Sematech is organized that will facilitate its reaching its goals. First among these is the long history of the involvement of the Defense Department with the private sector and especially with high tech industries. A close relationship exists between high tech firms, such as those of the semiconductor industry, and the armed forces. It is not uncommon for private firms in the defense industry to require their employees to satisfy the Defense Department's security clearance requirements before they are allowed to begin employment, since many of the projects they work on may be classified. Because many suppliers to the armed forces deal with products and information that are classified, there is a strong infrastructure in place that will facilitate a transition to the requirements of Sematech.

Second, the Pentagon involves itself with the organizational and operational structure of its suppliers. The Defense Department conducts regular audits of all its defense contractors, approving of expenditures and establishing organizational requirements that meet its criteria. Almost any product purchased by the armed forces must fulfill certain guidelines and meet certain standards, as prescribed by the Defense Department. These military specifications, otherwise known as MIL Specs, are infamous in the industry and a source of constant headaches for a firm's management. The task of Sematech as envisioned would follow this pattern established by the Pentagon. The fact that Sematech would take the relationship between the Pentagon and the private sector one step further—a partnership between both parties—is fortuitous for it builds on existing relationships and cultures.

For these two reasons the road for Sematech may be less bumpy. The necessary foundation on which a successful venture can be built is present. The personal, organizational, and historical relationships are strong enough to facilitate a smooth transition from oligopoly to partnership. Inherent in this proposition, however, is the task at hand. What, precisely, will Sematech attempt to accomplish? In a high tech industry this is not an easy answer. The semiconductor business is technology dependent. The success or failure of a firm is precipitated by the state of technology. The turnover in the manufacturing process is great; technology life is brief and superior management skill is necessary to orchestrate the various factors that ultimately determine the success or failure of a venture. The commitment to the success of Sematech from the private and public sectors and the financial backing it will receive over the next few years strengthen the chances that the venture's program can be executed to the satisfaction of the parties involved. Such success would be welcome news for the United States.

NOTES

1. Edwin O. Reischauer, *The United States and Japan* (Cambridge: Harvard University Press, 1970), p. 274.

2. Peter Waldman, "Sematech Rushes to Meet Japan Challenge," *The Wall Street Journal*, January 8, 1988.

3. John Kenneth Galbraith, *Economics in Perspective* (Boston: Houghton Mifflin Company, 1987), p. 293.

7

DYNAMIC MANAGEMENT

The economic dislocation of the past decade threatens America's future. No one anticipated in 1980 that the United States would experience a loss of competitiveness of alarming proportions in world markets, that the United States would transfer over $1 trillion to foreigners by way of a massive trade deficit, that the United States would become the world's net debtor nation, surpassing the foreign debts of Brazil and Mexico combined, that the stock market would reach unsustainable heights, threatening the financial markets, that the American banking system would incur unprecedented losses, and that the threat of protectionism would loom over the remainder of the decade.

The economic dislocation is a serious development born out of the inability of management to understand the nature of the challenge confronting it, to say nothing of the inadequate leadership from government officials. The economy of 1990 is a global economy that is technology and information dependent. The ability to anticipate change and to deal with new, significant, and fast change is the basis on which success is built. For the corporate officer, the consequences of the changes the business environment has encountered and the resulting challenges have been overwhelming.

DYNAMIC MANAGEMENT STRUCTURES

The effects of new, significant, and fast changes have left no business immune to disruption. The consequences of a series of new, significant, and fast changes, which we term disruptive changes, for an economy as a whole are clear: economic dislocation. The consequences for an individual firm are as important. The corporate officer needs to understand the costs of disruptive changes. One is the loss of profit and the other is the cost in arresting or reversing the loss. Too often managers have been unable to recognize a change as a disruptive change requiring immediate action to minimize both these sources of loss. Corporate America has been characterized by a failure either to restore profitability or to shut down the business lines facing the disruptive change. The demonstrated inability to minimize the losses during the past decade does not bode well for the next decade.

The continued incurment of these losses by all sectors of the economy serves to underscore the need to change managerial modes in use if the United States hopes to regain its lost eminent position in the world economy. The demands of world trade and the nature of the newly competitive business environment require an adequate management system. Since the end of the Second World War, the most widespread management system in the United States has been the static management system (see Figure 7.1). Characterized by a top-down chain of command in which specific tasks are assigned individual managers, static management is implemented through either control or implementation management.

Control management assumes that the future stems from the past. The underlying assumption here is that there will be a continuation of business-as-usual in the future. This system is appropriate when there is low turbulence and volatility in the marketplace. Indeed, control management predicts that the future will be like the present, except there will be more. Such a static view of the market is no longer adequate for the task at hand.

Implementation management, likewise, is based on past performance. This inward-looking management approach assumes

Figure 7.1
Static Management vs. Dynamic Management

Static Management	Dynamic Management
Control Management	Extrapolative Management
- Low turbulence. - Future will be like past.	- Future will be different than past. - Use past to predict/forecast future.
Implementation Management	Entrepreneurial Management
- Low turbulence. - Firm's history is sufficient in determining future. - Performance judged by quotas and historical standards.	- Business environment is characterized by random events. - Survival rests on ability to recognize and exploit opportunities as they arise.

Source: International Credit Monitor.

that the firm's own historical experiences are sufficient for determining its future. Thus, a system of quotas and historical standards governs production and evaluation. The performance of each unit is seen as a stand-alone separate from the whole.

The limitations of static management are evident: the firm operates in a reactive manner, anticipating low turbulence, insignificant change, not exploiting interrelationships among the firm's units, and failing to prepare for change. This was the world of the 1950s when America remained unchallenged. Western Europe was struggling to rebuild itself, as was Japan, the Soviet bloc nations did not participate in important trade with the outside world, and the developing world, most notably Taiwan, Hong Kong, Brazil, and Singapore, did not constitute serious competition for American industry. In such a world, the future was like the past, except more and more world trade was dominated by the United States.

In the wake of disruptive changes, however, the world has

become a different place. The firm—or nation, for that matter—that is unable to anticipate threats, recognize opportunities, develop new markets where none existed before, introduce new technology, develop new manufacturing processes, products, or applications of existing goods, faces reduced opportunities. The management structure in place must be able to respond to the changing world economy and demonstrate the flexibility required for the volatility that characterizes the business environment of today.

The firm that implements a dynamic management system can fare well in the future. There have been significant gains made at the Uruguay round of the GATT talks for the liberalization of trade. The continued cooperation among the Group of Five for the stabilization of exchange rates coupled with the continuing program of trade liberalization presents significant opportunities for corporate America. The danger, however, lies in the fact that the very forces that bring about opportunities are the forces that constitute disruptive changes. The corporate officer is thus left with no alternative: disruptive changes are the trends of the future and the successful implementation of dynamic management techniques will allow the firm to make opportunities out of potential threats.

Dynamic management is the most appropriate management system for a nation struggling to recover from economic dislocation. The ability of dynamic management to process information and assign tasks in a more efficient manner is the secret of its success. There are two kinds of dynamic management: extrapolative and entrepreneurial management. Both techniques reject the static management assumption that the past is the key to the future (see Figure 7.1). In a time when the globalization of business rests on a high degree of turbulence, disruptive change is the norm, and fundamental economic dislocation is not uncommon, a more anticipatory management system is required.

Extrapolative management is based on the assumption that a firm needs to look to the future, realizing there are threats to anticipate and opportunities to seize. The past performance of the firm is seen as a guide to the internal workings of the environment in which the firm operates. Trends can be identified, forecasts drawn, and the performance of competitors, changes in the marketplace, and the role of technology assessed in order to formulate more accurate forecasts about future behavior. The firm expects the future to be different from the past and the emergence of disruptive changes serves to confirm the need to anticipate these disruptions and identify the opportunities that emerge from the changed environment.

Entrepreneurial management assumes that disruptive changes are the norm and that the business environment is characterized by random events that can transform a firm's fortunes overnight. The very survival of a firm depends on its ability to capitalize on opportunities as they arise. The ability to identify new markets, innovate, and benefit from economies of scale and of scope in its operational functions will enhance a firm's opportunities. The relative stability and predictability of the business environment in the 1950s is a rare exception. The disruptive changes that began with the collapse of Bretton Woods are more in line with what can be reasonably expected.

Dynamic management, then, assumes that turbulence and disruptive changes present opportunities that capable management can exploit. The high degree of uncertainty in the more competitive world economy demonstrates the applicability of dynamic management. Anticipating change, dynamic management seeks to identify new markets, create new products, and develop the necessary innovations that will benefit from the new markets that will emerge from uncertainty. At the same time it is aware that unseen threats lie behind each corner and that failure to see the future for what it is can be very dangerous.

MANAGEMENT SKILLS

"What can be done to check [the] declining economic and political power [of the United States]?" asked Leonard Silk in the *New York Times* on April Fool's Day, 1988. The article enumerated several proposals for reversing the demise of the United States in the world arena. These ranged from tired platitudes, such as "increased productivity," to noting the fact that the American technological lead has "narrowed." Among these proposals, however, was a reference to two lectures given by Derek C. Bok, president of Harvard University, that reveal one of the structural shortcomings in the United States today. "Knowledge is crucial to economic growth in the post-industrial society, and the United States universities are the greatest suppliers of new scientific knowledge," Mr. Silk reported. The failure of American education is that there is "so much emphasis on finance and analytic skills rather than on manufacturing, and for relatively neglecting such fields as international business, the motivation of workers, government relations and production."[1]

The need to reassess the educational system that produces management professionals is an urgent task. The kind of manager that is necessary for the United States to compete internationally is not the kind of manager being trained at the nation's leading schools. Never before has the need for capable management been more urgent in corporate America. "To be trained as an *American* manager is to be trained for a world that is no longer there," observed Lester Thurow, dean of MIT's Sloan School of Management in early 1988.[2] Indeed, many believe that a world in which the United States dominates, as it did in the 1950s, is almost impossible.

The dilemma of trade must be resolved so that the optimal outcome among equals prevails. This requires not only the kind of international trade arrangements that encourage a global interdependence to the benefit of all nations, but also requires the kind of manager that is capable of flourishing in this new environment. As Lester Thurow believes, it is important to have the kind of manager that has been internationalized and can function successfully in the emerging global marketplace. The best way for corporate America to compete in the world economy is to nurture executives who are sophisticated and as comfortable in New Delhi as in New York. The traditional disdain for overseas assignments must be discarded and it is important to place an emphasis on linguistic ability. While English remains the dominant language of business, the executive who can communicate in the lingua franca will enjoy a competitive advantage. The positive impact of negotiating and speaking in the prevailing language translates into invaluable goodwill.

In the United States, likewise, executives who are well versed in the ways of foreign cultures can provide decisive insight into the psyches of foreign markets. This, in turn, will enable the firm to design strategic marketing plans that are more sensitive and effective. The direct benefit to the firm will be seen in the generation of more exports. An indirect benefit, moreover, will be seen when competing with foreign firms in the domestic markets. If corporate America understands how the Japanese do business, how they think, and how their culture prioritizes value systems, vital information will become available that can help domestic car producers compete in the United States. By the same token, if corporate America understands the culture of a third nation in which it is competing against the Japanese, it is in a better position to prevail in the marketplace. The integration of an export-driven firm is the best way corporate America can compete.

Inherent in this strategy is the need for sophisticated executives. Consider the example of the San Francisco-based telecommunications concern Pacific Telesis International. After several years of attempting to enter the international telecommunications market, this California firm has had only modest success, while incurring substantial losses. Its ambitious marketing plans have been reduced time after time and it has had to withdraw from important markets in Spain, Europe, the Pacific Rim, and Australia after meeting with failure. Its achievements have been modest both in scope and in revenues generated. A closer examination of the problems encountered by this start-up firm reveals the importance of Lester Thurow's advice that corporate executives must "have an understanding of how to manage in an international environment."[3] This lack of understanding has a detrimental impact on a firm's prospects. The lack of international experience among the directors at this firm contributed to its early demise. Most managers came from Pacific Bell, one of the regional baby bell companies created in connection with the break-up of AT&T, and few had any significant international experience. The kinds of skills required to rise through the ranks of a utility are different than what the new global marketplace requires. Several directors, for example, were college dropouts who worked their way up

in Pacific Bell before joining this new firm. The lack of prepa-
ration on the part of these officers contributed to the problems
encountered by this company. Among the Harvard MBAs
brought in to supplement the caliber of the "Bell Head" management team, there were problems as well. One director, for
example, was an individual who had foresaken a family life to
pursue a career and was so obsessed with shortcomings in her
career and in her inability to find time for social development
that this individual's work suffered and had a negative impact
on the start-up firm. In the next decade American society will
struggle to strike a balance between an individual's right to pri-
vacy and an individual's obligations to society, including his
employer. While the personal life of an executive officer is his
own affair, in cases where productivity is affected, it becomes
of importance to the firm. It cannot be denied that corporate
officers must be understanding of executives going through
personal problems, such as a divorce or drug dependency. At
the same time, however, prudent managers recognize that individuals who display a disturbing inability to establish a healthy
balance in their personal lives will undoubtedly transfer this
propensity for the extreme—whether in judgment or in work
habits—to their business lives. Unbalanced individuals are unbalanced executives. The social inadequecies of this director,
for example, explain to a large measure the reasons business
benchmarks were never reached. Another Telesis director, after
three dismal years of frustration and squandering hundreds of
thousands of dollars, was transferred back to Pacific Bell with
a significant cut in level and salary and said, "at least I saw the
world."[4] A revealing presence of pathos among the incompetent.

Those interested in "seeing the world" should join the navy,
not corporate America. The newly competitive business environment cannot afford to send the incompetent on world tours.
The business of America is business and not sightseeing. The
failure of this firm and the subsequent retrenchment reveal
strategic shortcomings in how top management is staffed. The
serious challenges faced by the United States require serious
men and women. The manager that may have been adequate
in years gone by is not the kind of manager that will survive

in the next century. The importance for the firm is fundamental because the individual strengths—and weaknesses—of an executive determine the fate of the firm. The absence of management excellence undermines attempts to regain lost market shares.

The alarming lack of executive talent is evident to foreigners. When a Japanese firm buys an American company, for example, it customarily implements a rigorous training program that, under the guise of smoothing the transition to a different "corporate culture," is really designed to increase the skills of its new American workers. Competence, after all, is not part of corporate culture. Foreign firms that overlook the need to upgrade the caliber of management skill run unnecessary risks. Consider the acquisition by the British firm Blue Arrow of Manpower. This transaction, which was valued at over $1 billion, was one of the largest purchases by a foreign firm of an American company in 1987. In the course of completing the acquisition Blue Arrow placed little emphasis on the management at Manpower and its subsidiaries. "This is a mistake," said Carlo Sensenhauser, an investment banker at a major Denver-based investment house. "If Blue Arrow expects to succeed in the United States," Mr. Sensenhauser observed, "it must address the management issue. The competitive environment in the United States today requires highly skilled managers who can rise above the mediocrity prevalent at Manpower's business units."[5]

The reason for this concern stems from the disappointing performance of some of Manpower's subsidiaries. Under the management of Joel Miller and Ann Blythe, the performances of some California subsidiaries have fallen below expectations. Problems that the employment services division of Manpower has experienced prolonged losses. "In the second quarter of 1987," Mr. Sensenhauser noted, "this division accomplished nothing but losing money." This is not the kind of management that Blue Arrow bargained for when it acquired Manpower. The difficulties encountered here are also tied in to the general lack of management skill evident in corporate America. "If Blue Arrow is to succeed in the United States," Mr. Sensenhauser argued, "it will need to reevaluate the management talent at its American subsidiaries. The dismal performance of Joel Miller and Ann Blythe at the helms of Manpower's California units reveals a tremendous lack of capable management skill at Blue Arrow's American units. The disappointing performance of some of its California business units indicates that a higher level of management skill is required if the British giant is to succeed in the United States. The new realities of the marketplace leave no room for mediocrity."[6] The ability of Blue Arrow to maximize its recent American acquisition will, in large part, determine if it will succeed in the competitive American market.

The structural deficiencies of inadequate management skill are painfully evident. The reason the United States has lost competitiveness in the world arena lies in the executive suites of corporate America. Long accustomed to a world with no significant competition, American business now struggles to regain lost market shares. The surge in exports, spurred to a large degree by the devalued dollar, sets the stage for implementing the strategic decisions necessary to sustain the momentum facilitated by the favorable exchange rates. The corporate executive must take advantage of this window of opportunity to implement effective management structures that will make the firm competitive in the new global arena.

NOTES

1. Leonard Silk, "Economic Scene," *New York Times*, April 1, 1988.
2. Lester Thurow, *Zero Sum Solution* (New York: Simon & Schuster, 1985), p. 34.
3. Ibid.
4. Steve Potter, telephone interview, February 20, 1987.
5. Telephone interview, May 10, 1988.
6. Ibid.

8

ECONOMIES OF SCALE AND SCOPE

Corporate America must redefine its operating systems. This recommendation is based on characteristics of market realities:

- Product life cycles are shorter. Market segmentation now requires a larger variety of products in smaller volumes. The consolidation in the food industry, for example, has not been reflected in the variety of consumer foods available. The soup section of any supermarket brings this home vividly; whereas in the 1950s the brand of soup that dominated the supermarket shelves was Campbell's, there are dozens of brand names today with hundreds of soups targeting specific markets.

- Process technologies are more sophisticated. The manufacturing process is technology dependent and the pace of change has intensified. The traditional factory is now outdated; assembly line work is being replaced by work that offers greater responsibilities to workers and a greater variety of tasks, but requires a higher level of work skills. As manufacturing incorporates robotics and high tech processes, fewer but more highly trained workers will reshape the traditional assembly line.

- Market turnover requires more flexible response time. As new products enter markets, as technology changes, and as new markets are created, it is vital for an organization to respond to the quickened pace of economic change. The rapid rate of technological change and product innovation requires firms to continue to shorten the time necessary to bring a product to market. The need to gather and analyze information will become greater. The lag in decision-making must be shortened. As firms enter a more competitive business environment, the need for the orderly processing of information must be met if a sustainable competitive advantage is not to be undermined.

The solution to this dilemma is the implementation of lines of expertise within a firm that will enable it to respond to the realities of the global economy. The internal organizational structure must change. In the course of implementing competitive strategies, the internal horizontal structure of the firm must reflect the new realities of the intensively competitive marketplace. The firm, intent on achieving related diversification through related lines of business, needs to establish the links from the start that maximize the interrelationships among the various business units.

The program for adopting a horizontal organizational structure is comprised of three parts: business unit interrelationships, economies of scale, and a new partnership between labor and management. The global business environment requires a renewed effort to establish "lines of expertise" that give the firm a distinct advantage in meeting the specific needs of the market niches it has identified. This requires a functional organizational structure that is sensitive to the potential benefits horizontal links represent and commitment to competitive strategies that complement the firm's culture and build on the strengths of management. In the same manner that the physical structure must reflect the needs of the international business environment, so must competitive strategies reflect the strengths of individual corporate officers and the intangible personal culture of the firm, its image to the outside world, its history, and the identity within the company.

The purpose is to secure a set of Strategic Business Units (SBUs) exploiting opportunities in related lines of business that can complement each other, thus resulting in a firm that is worth more than the sum of the unrelated business units were they to be stand-alone entities. That intangible synergy, that special essence is recognition of a distinctive expertise in a capacity that no other competitor can offer. The goal is to make the firm less vulnerable to forces outside its control, such as exchange rates or government action, while making the firm more responsive to changes in the global marketplace. The end result is a firm that offers a particular value to its customers' value chains that cannot be satisfied by any other firm, domestic or otherwise. Thus the internal structure of the firm determines whether the competitive strategies in place will bear fruit.

HORIZONTAL STRUCTURE

The uncertainty of what, if any, protectionist measures will be implemented by government and the uncertainty that GATT provisions will be strengthened interferes with normal economic activity. The emergence of a structural deficit economy in the United States, the stagnation experienced by many debt-ridden nations, and the lack of progress in establishing an enforcement mechanism to facilitate international trade have contributed to slower growth rates among the Western nations (see Figure 8.1). The lackluster economic growth of countries such as Japan and West Germany, for example, has angered Americans, for the slower domestic growth rates in these countries contribute to the inability of the United States to increase exports. The saturation of domestic markets in the United States and an uninspired economic growth rate result in more fierce competition for market shares among firms, squeezing corporate profit margins even further.

Under these circumstances, firms have had to shift their focus away from growth toward profits. The slower world growth rates could be addressed in two ways. First, new markets could be opened. China, the Soviet Union, and Brazil, for example, are nations that protect certain sectors of their economies. If these markets were opened to foreign firms, corporate America could increase exports to these markets, addressing the trade imbalance picture. Second, the mature Western economies and the debt-ridden developing nations could coordinate fiscal and monetary policies in order to encourage growth. These two avenues, however, are not promising in the short term; closed markets open very cautiously and attempts at coordination among the Western powers has had limited success. Therefore, the firm needs to focus on establishing quality market shares in which it can focus on profits. Profits, moreover, are best maximized through a program to establish competitive advan-

Figure 8.1
Annual Percent Change in Gross National Product of Selected Countries 1980–1985 and
1985–1986

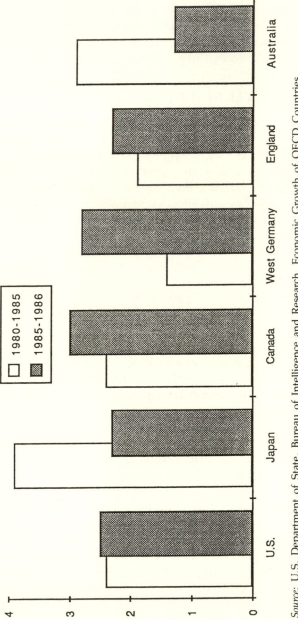

Source: U.S. Department of State, Bureau of Intelligence and Research, Economic Growth of OECD Countries,
1976–1986, *Report No. IRR 76 (Revised),* 1987.

tage. The reason for harnessing the impressive economic power of interrelationships is to lower costs, increase differentiation, and enhance marketing. The firm's competitive standing improves through these links among its business units in related lines of expertise. It is this emphasis on profit enhancement, however, that gives rise to the arguments in favor of related diversification.

Horizontal structure, moreover, is based on a long-term view of the firm's ultimate objectives in the global marketplace. Corporate strategies aimed at securing competitive advantage are at the root of strategic planning. This, in turn, implies that long-term competitive considerations play the central role in establishing interrelationships. The short-term issues concerning financial matters and shareholder views take a back seat to the firm's viability in the marketplace in the long run. This should come as no surprise. The emphasis on the long term is what accounts for the success of many foreign firms who have paid the price of patience in order to reach the enviable positions they now occupy. The West Germans and the Japanese came to dominate the global economy through a long-term strategy designed to create lines of expertise against which few American firms can compete effectively.

The first step in creating a horizontal structure is for the links among the business units to be structured in order to benefit from the economies of scale that are now possible. A natural outgrowth from these reinforced links is economies of scope. The flexibility offered by cutting across traditional divisional barriers between the business units gives rise to synergies which, when explored, contribute to superior performance. The economies of scope, moreover, complement the long-term requirements of strategic planning. In order to reap the benefits of competitive advantages, top management needs to allocate sufficient time for the economies of scope to become apparent. This requires not only a solid relationship with shareholders, but also a firm partnership between labor and management. The breach of trust that has occurred during the cost-cutting programs of the past decade must be mended. The damage done to morale among the rank and file and between business unit managers and executive officers must be repaired before an effective strategic planning program can be implemented throughout the firm.

BUSINESS UNIT INTERRELATIONSHIPS

An efficient program to establish links among the business units that benefit from the potential economies of scale requires the identification and selection of functions that are either standardized or benefit from volume purchases. The actual functions a firm targets for linking, of course, depend on the nature of its lines of business. Regardless of the functions selected, executive officers need to select functions that cut through business unit divisional barriers in order to maximize cost savings. There are, however, basic business functions that transcend industry and market considerations. The following are areas that should be selected for horizontal interrelationships:

- Administrative Services, Graphics. All printed matter, from business cards and stationery to posters and brochures, must be handled by one central department that serves the printing needs of all the business units.

- Administrative Services, Official Directory. The use of a central directory service for locating employees and updating phone lists, office numbers, mailing addresses, and related issues should be handled by a single office that serves the needs of the firm.

- Computer and Word Processing Services. A central computer and word processing division should be established for the typing and presentation requirements among the business units. One pool charged with using the Wang and Macintosh systems offers an optimal resource for the compilation of materials other than routine letters and memoranda.

- Corporate Communications. All communications to employees on company business—everything from company picnics to the procedures for filing W-2 forms—should be approved and produced by one center responsible for the distribution of all internal communiqués.

- Corporate Strategy. The planning, execution, and compliance functions of the firm's strategies must originate from one office. This way the firm can best monitor the progress of each business unit. This is necessary if problems and weaknesses are to be identified and solutions implemented in a short time span.

- Events and Receptions. The planning and hosting of dinners, receptions, and other events is best handled by a single office. For events other than informal functions among the employees within a business unit, the experience of a professional special events staff, familiar with available caterers and the requirements, is preferred.

- Federal/State Regulatory Services. The compliance with all federal and state laws should be monitored by one office. This function could be performed by either the human resource or legal service offices, depending on the lines of business in which the firm operates.

- Government Regulatory Services. One central division should monitor compliance with the trade, tariff, quota, duty, and customs requirements of domestic and foreign governments.

- Human Resources. The personnel needs of the entire firm must be handled by one office. This streamlines procedures, standardizes the procedures for hiring new employees, ensures that all the required paperwork is completed and identifies the availability of candidates seeking transfers and relocations within the firm. In addition, more specific functions must be consolidated into one central office:

    Benefit Plans Common to All. The negotiations of health, dental, and disability insurances can best be administered by the personnel office, billing costs on a per-employee and a per-participation basis to each business unit.
    Benefit Plans Common to Firm. The costs of operating a common human resources office should be distributed among the business units.
    Clerical and Secretarial Support. The allocation of clerks, secretaries, and receptionists can be operated according to the size of the firm. The larger company can benefit from a generic pool of support employees and can assign these employees to different business units on a temporary basis to replace employees who may be out ill, on vacation, or working on special projects requiring help in the short term.
    Executive Services. The special nonpecuniary benefits of top management should be handled by one office. In recent years such services as finanical planning and fitness programs, for example, have been afforded top management and these benefits should be the responsibility of one office.
    Hiring. The procedures for hiring employees and monitoring compliance with applicable labor laws and immigration issues should be coordinated by one central office.
    Office Space. The responsibility for securing adequate office space, entering into leases, subletting, and recommending office space projects must be administered by one central office that can monitor changes in the needs of the firm.
    Relocations/Transfers. Individuals willing to relocate or seeking transfers

can be matched up to opportunities in other business units through one central listing for the company. Such intracompany transfers and relocations save the costs of losing employees or hiring from outside to fill needs as they emerge.

- Legal Services. The legal requirements of the firm should be handled by one office in order to protect the firm. All legal matters need to originate from and be approved by one central office for consistency.

- Marketing and Sales. The marketing and sales functions of a similar nature can be linked. Firms operating in related lines of businesses can be expected to group complementary products into packages that can be sold as units to customers. The degree to which marketing and sales forces can be combined within a firm will vary greatly among different companies.

- Media and Public Relations. Official communications outside the firm and all inquiries from the public need to be cleared by a single office. The failure to approve of press releases, letters to the public and shareholders, and public statements can cause confusion and embarrassment if each business unit is allowed to operate on its own.

- Motor Vehicles. The management of company cars needs to be centralized to reduce the costs of automobile, van, and truck purchases, their maintenance, and the costs of leasing these vehicles to the business units.

- Planning Research Functions. The analysis of market trends, shifts in customer profiles, competitor moves that affect the industry, and the continual evaluation of what strategic and policy changes are necessary for the business units to accomplish their mission is best handled by a single office.

- Primary Materials and Input. The bulk purchase of basic inputs, such as computer memory chips, resistors, and capacitors for high tech business units, that several business units require plays a pivotal role in reducing production costs and should be the responsibility of the specific business unit.

- Procurement Functions. The procurement functions not related directly to the manufacturing process but necessary for the smooth operation of offices needs to be handled by one office. These functions are:

  Contracts. The proper maintenance of an office requires certain maintenance functions the building leasing company may not handle. These range from companies that provide bottled drinking water, to vending machine

maintenance, to flower arrangements for reception areas, to the maintenance of office plants, to carpet cleaning.

Mail and Messenger Services. In order for the business units to qualify for
volume discounts with overnight and overseas carriers and local messenger services their businesses may have to be consolidated into a single
account with different pick-up and drop-off points handled by a company-
wide office responsible for overseeing these functions.

Office Supplies and Furniture. The bulk purchase of all office supplies,
from copy machine paper and legal pads to pens and binders, must be
handled by one office. The same office should keep the inventory of office
furniture—from desk lamps and chairs to framed prints and sofas—in order to purchase in large quantities and maintain an accurate inventory of
the company's business units.

- Technology Transfer. A business unit may have a ready-made market by selling its products to other units requiring them. A business
unit that manufactures printed circuit boards, for example, may be
able to sell its services to several other business units that require
circuit boards as part of their products. In this way, a duplication in
technological and manufacturing processes among the business units,
or "reinventing the wheel," does not exist. A firm should not overlook the "hidden" markets that may exist among the business units.

- Technology Development. It is apparent that a firm whose business
units are diversified in related lines of products and services are
complementary in the sense that they satisfy several points on their
customers' value chain. Thus, as the emphasis on technology and
innovation becomes more evident in disturbed economic times, the
need to have but one technology development center becomes crucial to the firm's success. In the years ahead technology will take
center stage in strategic planning processes and the formulation of
competitive strategies across all industries.

- Travel. In order to keep travel and entertainment expenses within
company guidelines one office should be charged with selecting the
services, whether for air carriers, hotels, car rentals, or restaurants,
that are approved. This does not imply that unit personnel are not
allowed to make plane reservations themselves, but rather that they
must use the approved travel agencies, stay at the hotels, rent from
the car rental firms, and dine at the restaurants that are mandated
by the firm.

The economies of scale made possible by incorporating these
functions in the services shared among the firm's business units
are great. The costs should be billed to the business units in

two ways. For services provided by the firm that constitute overhead, such as corporate strategy and technology development functions, funding should come from all the business units as determined by a standard formula. The costs involved in administering these functions should be billed on an equitable basis with a proportional share of the expense of services rendered to all the business units. For services that are user dependent, such as office supplies and word processing work, each unit should be billed to reflect the actual service provided. The cost of providing these services needs to be on a per-use basis in order for units to remain within their budgets.

The object of exploiting business unit interrelationships is to reduce costs through the combined procurement of basic services. The monetary cost savings that are realized through such economies of scale have an added benefit for the firm, however. The role the corporate officers play in providing these functions to their units allows for a more careful surveillance of developments that can affect the competitive strategies of the firm. It is necessary to keep a constant monitor on the activities of the units, changes in the marketplace, and the actions of a company's competitors if threats and opportunities are to be identified in a timely fashion. The rate of technological innovation and the emergence of new products is increasing; competitive strategies must therefore reflect a heightened awareness of the implication these changes represent and that strategies based on the preservation of the status quo are futile.

There are, however, opportunity costs of engaging in the interrelated activities discussed above. The firm faces the administrative costs inherent in the process of coordinating these services among the business units. At the same time there are costs arising from the need for consistency. The firm has to establish a pattern of behavior that is consistent in order to establish cycles that can be analyzed. This involves engaging in functions that are suboptimal; for example, it may be necessary to buy a basic input in a given quantity that the units cannot process in a timely fashion, thus incurring the additional costs of coordinating production schedules among the business units or the costs of storing the surplus materials. It is easy to see the need for managers to compromise here and there in order to find a sustainable equilibrium. The inevitable gaps that emerge constitute the opportunity costs of implementing horizontal links throughout the organizational structure. Thus, the costs of coordination and consistency must be overall lower than the actual benefits derived from the economies of scale on which interrelationships are built.

These costs, fortunately, are very much a factor of the nature of the interrelationships developed by the firm. In the recommendations made above, these functions by and large transcend timing considerations. While primary input, procurement effort, and marketing efforts require considerable timing, negotiation, and compromise among the units, most of the other services do not. Motor vehicle maintenance, the purchase of paper clips, and the majority of the functions identified can occur in a consistent manner that requires little, if any, compromise among the business units. Therefore, the costs of coordination and consistency rise depending on how complementary the related lines of business are in which the units engage. Since these vary from firm to firm, it is safe to say that the challenge lies in maximizing the benefits of business unit interrelationship to promote efforts to adopt horizontal structures.

HORIZONTAL ECONOMIES OF SCOPE

The creation of links that are based on cultivating the benefits derived from the various interrelationships that exist among the firm's business units is appropriate for today's competitiveness. The proper use of economies of scale leads to economies of scope. There has been much debate over the ability to think of economies of scope in a tangible manner, but it is important to recognize that while the benefits derived from economies of scope cannot be measured in the same concrete terms as those of economies of scale, they are of significance to the company's overall performance.

The intangible nature of horizontal economies of scope does not reduce its benefits to the corporate entity. The idea contained in this discussion of economies of scope is in the observation that the single most important asset any firm has in its

efforts to establish a competitive advantage is its human resources. It is the abilities of its managers, the vision of its leaders, the lines of command, power, and influence within the
organization that shape the kinds of expertise the company cul-
tivates. Unless the top officers recognize the intangible benefits
derived from the expertise of their managers, no set of competitive strategies can be expected to accomplish its goals.

The introduction of a horizontal organizational structure presents the opportunity to cut across traditional divisional barriers. This gives rise to certain economies of scope based on the
intangible benefits that come from expertise, know-how, and
experience. The qualities, which cannot be measured, are the
decisive elements in determining which firm will succeed in
securing and defending a market leadership position. The objections to thinking about the effects of these horizontal economies of scope overlook the importance the expertise and character of a firm's managers play in fostering confidence,
motivating the rank and file, and presenting an image to the
outside world about the nature of a firm's intentions.

These intangibles—expertise, know-how, and experience,
which are enhanced through business unit interrelationships,
are the basis for assessing the competence of management. Here
again the substance of the subjective appraisal of an intangible
quality such as competence presents a series of challenges.
Nevertheless, in the same manner that economists are able to
make accurate calculations about consumer behavior through
revealed preferences, so can various levels of competence be
determined through revealed behavior. The ability of managers
to overcome obstacles, implement their policies, assess the economic and business environment, and triumph in the marketplace all speak of an individual manager's or management team's
traits. The competence level of a firm's management, moreover, can be determined through the evaluation of observed
behavior in the marketplace.

An assessment of how developed the horizontal economies
of scope are in a firm can be determined through the examination of the men and women in charge as well as the procedures in practice. These are:

- Manager Ability. The ability of a manager to respond constitutes his level of competence. A manager who demonstrates resistance to change undermines his ability to function in the context of increased competition and world economic turbulence. It is not sufficient to assess past track records because the ability to function under a given level of turbulence or within the defined parameters of a specific industry does not guarantee that the same level of competence can be expected in a higher or lower level of turbulence or in a line of business that is removed from his area of expertise.

- Horizontal Problem-Solving Process. There are different levels of scope to be realized through the problem-solving procedures in place in any given organization. The fact, however, remains that problem-solving procedures based on historical performance are less effective in times of turbulence than procedures that attempt to create innovative alternatives when possible or those that attempt to select an optimal mix chosen from a set of alternatives that are based on proven experiences of the business units. The firm that moves away from an emphasis on precedents and seeks innovations instead will meet with greater success.

- Management Structure. The kind of management structure required to exploit the benefits of economies of scope is Dynamic. Competitiveness in the new global marketplace cannot occur unless the expertise of a firm's managers is geared to using extrapolative or entrepreneurial management styles. These management structures are forward looking and thus seek to anticipate future threats, opportunities, and changes that stand to affect the fundamental structure of an industry or market. The specific and unique know-how of individual corporate officers lends itself to the widespread use of management aimed at solving problems through extrapolative techniques that can quantify the effects of a threat, the possibilities of an opportunity, or the implications of industry and market changes.

- Information Process. It is easy to understand that to implement a management structure capable of influencing the future and not relegated to responding to events in the marketplace the role information plays is most important. The process by which information is collected, analyzed, and managed determines to what degree the firm will be able to control its own destiny. The best approach that can enhance economies of scope throughout the entire company is an information process that relies on the extrapolation of information from the performance of each business unit and each project while keeping a constant vigil over factors that affect the business environment and economic context of the appropriate areas in which a firm operates. To accomplish this requires management with a solid hands-on experience in the processes of using information and incorporating these into competitive strategies. The ability of managers to compete against competitors is enhanced by a shrewd awareness of the developments that foreshadow change.

- Organizational Limits. The ability to benefit from these economies of scope is limited only by the degree to which interrelationships are developed. The higher the level of horizontal organization the greater the capacity for the firm to handle the volume and the complexity of the strategic requirements. A firm needs to be responsive to market realities and adapt to changes if it is to survive. Thus, the kind of manager that can deliver valuable economies of scope to the firm demands an environment that rewards creative and innovative approaches to business. The implied risk taking must be explicitly encouraged and measures to ensure that the organizational structure of the firm can handle the effects of creativity and risk must be in place. This, then, alludes once again to the need to replace short-term with long-term considerations. Unless there is a commitment to a solid set of competitive strategies, the managers responsible for the success of a business unit or a project will grow restless with the perceived impatience. To avoid potential turnover the firm's organizational structure must reflect the long-term considerations.

- Positional Responsibilities. The final component that determines how much a firm can expect to benefit from the know-how and experience of its corporate officers centers on the way positional responsibilities are defined by top management.

In dynamic environments encouraging extrapolative and entrepreneurial styles, creativity and innovations are seen as the foundations of market leadership. In no uncertain terms, then, positions are defined in a manner that reflects the importance of risk, innovation, and a broader sense of freedom to develop insights that can enhance competitive strategies. This requires, in part, a commitment to change and the offering of technological support to managers. In today's business environment, for example, inhouse desktop publishing for presentations and developments of strategies is a requisite to a sound program of strategic planning. The sense of control afforded managers who have access to the proper equipment and an official blessing to *think* about the company's lines of business, the firm's long terms, the implications of market developments, and how to develop strategies that reflect all these considerations is a bonus no firm can afford to pass up.

The importance of horizontal economies of scope lies in the ability to encourage a long-term perspective that is the foundation of developing sustainable international competitive strategies. To be sure, lack of foresight and ill-conceived strategies are to blame for the economic dislocation of the past decade. Not unlike other countries in the nineteenth century that committed similar errors, the United States has for too long relied on parochial views and myopic strategies. This must change. The necessary changes, however, can only come about through a concerted effort to implement the structural changes that can make use of economies of scope and to recruit managers that have a proven track record and show promise.

The reason economies of scope are of significant value to the firm is that only when the necessary structure is in place and the individuals with the right kind of expertise and know-how are available can two functions be performed: the identification of inputs to protect the firm and the fine tuning of competitive strategies to reduce vulnerability. Although it is difficult to measure the benefits of horizontal economies of scope to the corporation, they do exist as decisive elements in a manager's abilities and skills. If corporate America is to succeed in the highly competitve global marketplace, then managers who can address these two issues need to be identified, recruited, and cultivated.

PART IV

Implementing Trade Strategies

There are ample opportunities for corporate America to implement the management strategies discussed above. There is little doubt that these strategies can bear fruit and can contribute
to the nation's efforts to regain international competitiveness.
Indeed, despite doubts harbored by many, there are more opportunities for the United States today than there have ever
been in its history. As the economy has developed and changed,
two sectors have emerged as important growth areas for the
future: service and high technology. These are the natural
strengths of the United States. As the salariat economy ma-
tures, a great emphasis will be placed on the service industry,
and as technology advances, high tech will command a greater
importance in the national economic life of the United States.

The following case studies focus on these two industries. The
first case study is on the vacation cruise industry. The continuing growth in this industry offers ample opportunities to
American companies. while the analysis reveals a period of over
capacity in the short term, ambitious marketing can compensate for this weakness while positioning individual firms in a

way that enhances the long-term market dynamics of the industry. The second case study is on the semiconductor industry. Technological innovation as well as industry efforts to create a unique partnership program between the private and public sectors in the form of Sematech reveal how the United States can adapt to the new realities of the marketplace and to the demanding nature of the economies of scale mandated by the investment requirements of high technology. These two case studies reinforce the argument that there are opportunities out there. Corporate America is more than capable of establishing a formidable presence in these, as well as other, industries.

9

THE CRUISE INDUSTRY: A CASE STUDY

While American manufacturers have made considerable gains in international trade thanks to a weaker dollar and state-of-the-art facilities, it is important to recognize the vast opportunities that lie in other industries. The service industries stand to make a considerable contribution to American efforts to establish sustainable market shares in the world economy. The following case study is an analysis of the cruise industry. As leisure time increases and the competitiveness of cruises relative to other forms of vacations is enhanced, there will be a significant rise in the demand for cruise vacations. Vacations are an excellent export product, for they constitute a service not readily available in all nations. Try as you might there are no beaches as warm as those in the Caribbean anywhere in Iceland, which is why people from Iceland who wish to "import" a tropical vacation need to physically go to the Caribbean.

As the economy readies to enter the twenty-first century, the services sector will dominate and in so doing will become the focus of America's drive to ameliorate its balance of trade position. The cruise industry was chosen for this case study for another reason. There are currently significant plans for expansion by the major cruise lines that will result in a temporary oversupply in the early 1990s. The challenges this oversupply of space poses for the strategic plans of the major cruise lines is of no small importance. There will be several years when aggressive marketing, significant discounting, and responsive strategic plans will be required if each firm of the cruise industry is to increase—let alone maintain—its market share. The current expansion underway presents a great opportunity for individual firms within the cruise industry to become leaders of international importance. The cruise market is changing as American demographics change, and the devalued dollar will increase the number of foreigners who constitute a significant potential market for the cruise lines. The changing preferences among young people of college age, moreover, stand to influence the kinds of vacation packages offered. Whether or not the cruise industry can make a significant contribution to American efforts to improve service exports will depend on the caliber of managers and strategic planners that various firms employ.

INDUSTRY MARKET DEMAND

The demand for cruise vacations is generated by two market segments: experienced cruisers and potential first-time cruisers. This is no great revelation, as the demand models designed for the cruise industry illustrate (see Figure 9.1). The first market segment consists of people who have already taken a cruise. It takes into account such variables as age, the addition of new experienced cruisers, vacation alternatives, and mortality. Fluctuations in the demand generated by this market segment depend on economic conditions, rates for repeat cruisers, meeting the demands of repeat cruisers, and the destination alternatives offered. The demand generated by experienced cruisers for cruise industry services has increased in absolute terms. In the next decade the majority of cruisers will be repeat cruisers. As a result, cruise lines will have to cater to the demands of the experienced cruisers, for they will dominate the demand for the industry's product.

The second market segment, potential first-time cruisers, consists of individuals who have not taken cruises but meet the age, income, and lifestyle profile of cruisers. The total size of this market is, quite naturally, a function of demographics, pre-

Figure 9.1
Demand Model Structure for Cruise Industry

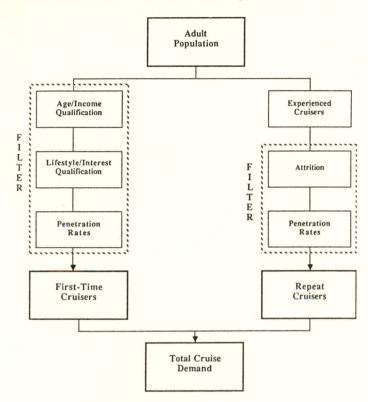

Source: International Credit Monitor.

vailing economic conditions, and the appeal of the characteristics of the cruise product. The demographics of the general population reveal two trends. First, the busy schedules of two-professional households, for example, has contributed to a sharp increase in demand for short vacations. The three- and five-day vacations are preferred over the traditional two-week vacation of yesteryear. The demands on the time of many professionals prevent many married professionals from both having two weeks off at the same time. The result has been a demand for shorter, but more frequent, miniature vacations. The cruise-line industry needs to cater to the demands of middle-aged working professionals. Another demographic trend is the increasing demand for cruise services by retired individuals. People are living longer and are more active in their later years. This, coupled with their relative affluence, accounts for the sharp increase in demand for cruise services by the older segments of the general population. Retired couples traveling together often opt for the longer cruise packages, preferring a more leisurely vacation where the pace is slower, there are more ports of call, and there is a wide selection of on-board activities.

The prevailing economic conditions also affect the number of potential first-time cruisers. If the entry price of cruises is reduced, then a larger percentage of the total population that could afford a cruise rises. Thus, while the prices of cruise products have remained stable over the past few years, the significant dollar devaluation has made cruise services far more economical for Europeans. In the past the cruise industry has resorted to price discounting to increase the total number of passengers. Sound strategies would try to avoid any discounting over the next few years. The devalued dollar represents an opportunity to tap the European market. The number of Europeans coming to America has increased significantly since 1985. The attraction of Florida as a vacation destination for Europeans has increased. Many Europeans are taking advantage of the weak dollar to take their children to Disney World and Epcot Center. Since the Caribbean dominates the cruise industry, tourism to the United States from Europe constitutes a significant pool of potential first-time cruisers.

The appeal and characteristics of the cruise service are the final components of demand. The lifestyles of potential first-time cruisers play a significant role in shaping the cruise programs offered. Attempts to appeal to a broader market have resulted in a new emphasis on meeting the demands of the younger end of the market. More cruise lines are offering sports and fitness programs in conjunction with shorter cruises. Young professionals, for example, prefer shorter cruises with programs emphasizing health-conscious activities, such as aerobics and swimming. These couples prefer to leave Miami, Los Angeles, or New York on three- or five-day cruises to destinations such as the Bahamas, Baja California, or Bermuda, respectively. In contrast, the older end of the market segment is more concerned with leisure activities and a longer cruise. Cruise itineraries that include more exotic ports of call and require a longer time are of greater interest to this market segment. Whereas younger couples may wish to take a month-long cruise around South America, it is the older market segment that has enough time to do so. Strategic plans for the cruise lines must include service differentiation for these distinct but important market segments.

The demand for cruise services is a function of the interplay of experienced cruisers and potential first-time cruisers. The cruise industry needs to cater to the demands of the repeat cruiser, who will become the typical cruiser in the years ahead, and at the same time it must entice sufficient potential first-time cruisers in order to increase the pool of experienced cruisers. This is important, for the oversupply in the years ahead will make the cruise lines more dependent on the repeat cruiser to sustain occupancy at its present levels. The demand for cruise services, however, is also influenced by several factors outside the control of the cruise industry. Alternative travel choices and general economic dynamics influence the total potential first-time cruiser pool as well as the readiness of experienced cruisers to take another cruise. The total strength of demand, however, is ultimately a function of the market dynamics affecting the cruise industry.

MARKET DYNAMICS

The use of tourism as a source of hard currency and to offset trade imbalances has a long history with many developing nations. The United States also has the potential of making use of tourism to improve its trade picture. For every American who decides to take a cruise in lieu of going abroad the trade balance is improved. This is so because going overseas is importation of a service. Although this may not be apparent at first, Americans who vacation in Europe are importing tourist services. The cruise industry can play a significant role in influencing how a vacation dollar is spent by the general population. At the same time, foreigners who vacation in the United States are the recipients of American service exports. The devaluation of the U.S. dollar since 1985 has created a surge of tourist service exports to Europeans and the Japanese. The cruise industry would do well to tap this market to enhance its position in the vacation market and to expand the pool of experienced cruisers.

The market, then, is a dynamic product of several forces. These are: economics of the day, competing travel alternatives, prevailing exchange rates, and appeal of destinations. Each of these factors shapes the total availability of potential first-time cruisers and the propensity of experienced cruisers to choose the cruise alternatives. The cruise industry can do very little to shape these market dynamics, but it is able to have contingency plans and marketing strategies that anticipate threats and exploit opportunities for its benefit. The expected rise in supply of cruise services and the uncertainty of the prevailing exchange rates necessitate an aggressive strategy that ensures there will be a significant increase in the pool of experienced cruisers over the next few years.

Economics. The overall economic conditions prevailing in any given year directly affect the disposable income of the general population. Cruise services, being a discretionary item, are affected by the rise or fall in the fortunes of the economy. During periods of expansion, the demand for cruise services rises without any hesitation. During times of uncertainty, the rise is more cautious. The American economy will muddle along with low growth as it has for most of the past decade. The relative stability this offers is comforting for it strengthens the chances that the conservative growth estimates made in this analysis are accurate.

Travel Alternatives. The ultimate demand for cruise services depends on the number of travel alternatives. The cruise industry must offer a vacation option of comparable value that can compete against the airline and hotel industry packages. The awareness in the public mind of the vacation value of cruise services is an important consideration for the traveling public. The recent trend of fare wars among the airlines constitutes stiff competition for the market segment able to plan ahead.

The cruise industry must be prepared to remain price competitive without resorting to steep discounting.

Exchange Rates. The dollar devaluation vis-à-vis the currencies of the other industrial nations is an opportunity for the cruise industry. The weaker dollar in Europe has reduced the number of Americans traveling to Europe while increasing the number of Europeans coming to the United States. This represents two opportunities for the cruise industry. First, more Americans will be vacationing at home, thereby increasing the pool of potential first-time cruisers. Second, the presence of foreign tourists in the United States enhances the ability of the cruise lines to market their services to Europeans planning their vacations. At the same time, the fact that the dollar has not fallen vis-à-vis the currencies of Mexico and developing nations in the Caribbean means that the purchasing power of potential first-time cruisers to tropical destinations has not been eroded, thereby adding to the attraction of a cruise.

Ports of Call. The total number of destinations offered by the cruise lines is a powerful determinant of demand. The ability of cruise lines to include attractive ports of call in their itineraries can constitute a competitive advantage. The potential first-time cruiser can be enticed more readily when there is a wide variety of destinations in any single cruise. Alternative travel packages may not be as varied or offer the convenience of an ocean vessel. Marketing strategies aimed at the older end of the market segment can make use of the more flexible schedules of this market. Itineraries for the younger end of the market can in turn offer attractive vacation alternatives for the hurried lifestyles of two-professional households. The marketing of ports of call can be an effective tool to increase penetration rates of potential first-time cruisers.

The market dynamics of the cruise industry lend themselves to aggressive marketing plans. The extent to which there is a service awareness among the general population depends on the marketing programs in place. The role of marketing will increase in the next five years precisely because the supply of cruise ships will increase. Since the industry will soon be in a period of oversupply, the prosperity of the individual cruise lines will depend on how successful they are in making sure that both experienced and potential first-time cruisers are aware of the services they offer and the value a cruise represents relative to other vacation alternatives. The use of intensive advertising, travel agent support and incentives, and service marketing are all necessary if an individual cruise line is to defend its current market position in the early 1990s.

INDUSTRY MARKET SUPPLY

The base case assumptions for the cruise industry project a 10 percent increase in the general population's interest and awareness of cruise services between 1988 and 1995; a 5 percent increase in the North American and European potential first-time cruise penetration rates; and a 1 percent increase in the experienced cruiser penetration rate. In total number the cruise demand generated by Americans, Canadians, and Europeans is expected to exceed 3 million by 1995 (see Figure 9.2).

This represents sustained growth in demand for cruise services, but at a slower rate than experienced between 1975 and 1985. This analysis assumes that the average cruise length will remain at 7.0 days and 355 operating days per berth per year with an occupancy rate of 80 percent of all available berths. The required increase in supply to meet the expected growth reflects these figures. The number of additional passengers between 1988 and 1995 is estimated to be 1,350,000. Assuming the current 80 percent occupancy rate will remain constant, then the projected demand will require the addition of 33,750 berths.

The supply of berths continues to grow. Since 1985 the number of berths has increased from 45,000 to 55,000. There are approximately 20,000 additional berths on order with delivery dates extending from the present through mid-1991. The delivery of these berths by 1991, coupled with the expected addition of another 21,000 berths through acquisition of new and existing ships, will result in a total capacity approaching almost 100,000 berths by 1995.

This poses an oversupply problem. Total cruise passenger volume is projected to exceed just over 3.3 million by 1995. This requires approximately 97,000 berths to meet the demand. The total supply of nearly 100,000 by 1991, however, means an

Figure 9.2
Historical and Projected Cruise Industry Passenger Volume 1978–1996

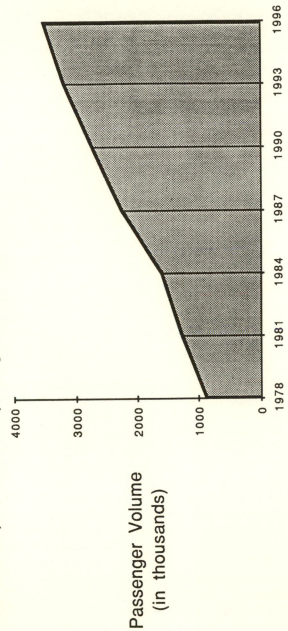

Passenger Volume
(in thousands)

Source: CLIA.

Historical figures suggest a 10 percent annual growth rate in passenger volume well into the 1990s.

excess supply from 1991 through 1995. In the early 1990s, then, cruise lines will most likely have problems filling up the required 80 percent of their berths. This excess supply will put great pressure on many cruise lines to implement discount programs and a reduction in load factors. The industry norm of 80 percent occupancy cannot be sustained in the early 1990s if no strategic plans of widespread importance are carried out. The industry as a whole will need to become more competitive vis-à-vis travel alternatives and respond to the changing demographics in order to have a larger pool of experienced cruisers it can target. This analysis expects that by 1995 the majority of passengers will be experienced cruisers and the average cruise length will decline from its current 7.0 days to approximately 6.2 days. The competitive strategies of the firms within the industry must reflect the challenges the potential oversupply demonstrates. The role of strategic plans for cruise lines must reflect the realities of the expected downturn in the industry in the early 1990s that the excess supply is expected to produce.

EXPORTING CRUISE SERVICES

Notwithstanding the temporary oversupply in the cruise industry, the export of cruise services stands to play a significant role as the United States addresses the problems of its trade imbalance. The traditional emphasis has been on traded goods but the service sector can play a vital role in assuring that the economic dislocation of the past decade is reversed. There are vast opportunities for the cruise industry today. The strong domestic growth in demand that is expected through 1995 is a firm foundation from which to launch an aggressive campaign to increase the pool of experienced cruisers long before the delivery of additional berths results in an oversupply. Along the way, the cruise industry can take the initiative and target a European market that already plans to import U.S. vacation services.

The most effective way of capitalizing on both the need to expand the pool of experienced cruisers and the market segment of the traveling European community is through an

Figure 9.3
Cruise Demand: North American Cruise Destinations

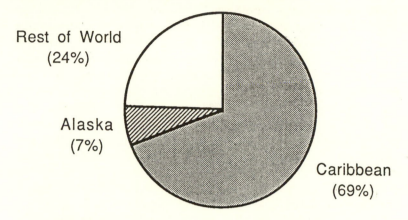

Rest of World
(24%)

Alaska
(7%)

Caribbean
(69%)

Source: Cruise Line Industry of America, Travel Pulse.

> Caribbean destinations continue to be the most popular within the cruise
> industry, accounting for almost 70% of North American demand and
> over half of all worldwide demand.

analysis of cruise destinations today. The Caribbean and Alaska
account for almost 80 percent of the American and Canadian
demand for cruises (see Figure 9.3). These two destinations account for approximately 50 percent of the world demand for
cruises. Thus, there is a natural advantage from which to build
a stronger pool base. The geographic proximity of the United
States to destinations in the Caribbean and the Alaskan coast
constitutes a natural marketing program that enables America
to develop a sustainable competitive advantage.

The cruise industry needs to implement an aggressive program that recognizes the opportunities the circumstances of the
day present and must anticipate the danger posed by a temporary oversupply. Indeed, only when a broad-based marketing program is in place can cruise services play an important
role in making significant inroads among European tourists and
American potential first-time cruisers to expand the present base
of experienced cruisers.

Product Differentiation

The geographic proximity of the United States to the highly sought after destinations in the Caribbean gives American cruise lines an advantage. The concept of a cruise as a total vacation alternative has to be defined in the public mind and marketed as a desirable choice among the various travel options. The most effective manner of accomplishing this is through an advertising campaign that highlights the completeness of cruising. The travel destinations to tropical ports of call with ideal climates, proximity to the American mainland, and the widespread use of English in the area strengthen the appeal of the Caribbean as a choice among potential first-time cruisers. The cruise industry needs to educate the public about the various destinations within the Caribbean it serves.

Once an underlying educational advertising campaign is completed, the industry can focus on product differentiation. In this service industry the kind of product differentiation that is needed is one that distinguishes between the requirements of the present and evolving market segments. As things stand today, the typical cruise lasts 7.0 days. This means that the criteria of the older end of the market segment and the traditional younger segment are being met. The typical cruise is out at sea for a week touring all the ports of call on its itinerary. This is a fine strategy, but the new demographics of the two-professional household requires an appropriate response to the needs of busy professional couples who do not have the luxury of taking the traditional two-week vacation time in one shot.

Therefore, marketing strategies must emphasize the need to cater to the time limitations of a growing market segment. This requires shorter cruises that last three to five days. For all practical purposes these are glorified extended weekends—which is precisely what the two-professional household seeks. Once an appropriate itinerary that caters to this market segment is established, the cruise line can begin an extensive campaign to educate the potential first-time cruisers about the different cruise options available for the different criteria of the various market segments. The cruise lines that can devise cruises of significantly shorter length than is the median today will have a marketing advantage in terms of enhancing the penetration rates for potential first-time cruisers. The Carnival line has been very successful in catering to the three-day cruises the affluent, busy, two-professional household prefers. The popular television advertisement campaign has worked well in getting name recognition among the general population. Other cruise lines, such as Royal Caribbean, have lagged in taking the initiative and implementing marketing plans that recognize the different needs of various market segments.

Cost Advantage

The price elasticity of demand for cruises is a problematic area. In the past, cruise lines have resorted to price discounting to fill berths when there was a need to stimulate demand. The problem, however, stems from the fact that when firms resort to discounting, the marginal net income is almost nonexistent. There is an insufficient markup in the cruise industry to sustain price discounting over an extended period of time. The result is that attempts to seek a cost advantage usually are short lived, result in no significant increase in net revenues, and establish a disturbing precedent that may affect the propensity of experienced cruisers to return to that line. The use of price discounting is not recommended because it cannot be justified and it does not contribute to net revenues.

Market Focus

The decision not to resort to price discounting as a marketing strategy complements specialized market focuses. The differentiation in the market segments lends itself to the targeting of specific programs designed to meet the criteria of the passenger profiles of each segment. The older, retired market segment is characterized by greater travel flexibility, leisure, and the desire for longer cruises. Most of these individuals travel in couples and with friends, are active, and prefer the combination of the traditional ports of call with the more exotic, such as a Caribbean cruise that includes ports of call on the Brazilian coast. The criteria of these passengers differ from other groups.

While they are active, they are not into physically strenuous regimes or sports. In contrast with other market segments there is a greater emphasis on social affairs and traditional dances. The cruise industry presently has effective programs that cater to the needs of this group and affords them the kind of cruise they prefer. The bulk of the experienced cruisers in this category can be counted on to be repeat cruisers within seven years of their last cruise. Except for mortality, they will constitute a significant portion of the passenger volume in 1995. Another market segment is the younger end of the market, the singles. These individuals, just entering the work force and recent college graduates, have more active lifestyles and demand social functions where they can meet other unattached singles in a relaxed setting. Their lifestyles demand more strenuous physical activities, such as aerobics and rock video dancing. There are cruise lines that cater to the need for social functions that incorporate the requirements of this group. There are, however, two additional groups that have been overlooked in the past. These are the two-professional households that have considerable time constraints. These individuals, often leaving their children in the care of relatives, wish to make time for each other where they can relax and do something out of the ordinary for three or five days. The relative affluence of this group is of consideration for they are willing to pay a premium for the peace and quiet they seek. The other group is just beginning to emerge and stands to prove a fertile market segment for the lean years anticipated in the early 1990s. These are college students. The natural limitations on their budgets mandate short trips. The decline of Ft. Lauderdale as a Spring Break destination, for example, offers opportunities to take these young individuals to other ports of call for three days. Often seeking areas that have lower drinking age laws, these individuals are willing to indulge in a three- or four-day cruise to the Bahamas or nowhere just for the thrill of the cruise. There are no reliable profile studies of the needs of this group, but their growing affluence and rise in numbers cannot be ignored.

The cruise industry is positioned to make significant contributions to this nation's efforts to reverse the state of affairs in its trade balance. There are vast opportunities to expand the total pool of experienced cruisers that will facilitate two goals. The first is to make cruising an attractive travel option that few potential first-time cruisers can pass over when compared with the alternatives. The second is to appeal to the European tourist who is already taking advantage of the low U.S. dollar to come to this country.

All the elements for success are there. The U.S. cruise industry is now positioned to make significant inroads into the international cruise industry. While the American lines already command a respectable share of the world market, the devaluation of the U.S. dollar and the proximity to the most dynamic cruise destinations indicate that the future is bright. Here is an entire industry poised to turn the trade picture around. Here is an opportunity for the United States to rack up important trade surpluses in the service sectors of the economy.

The future of the cruise industry is indeed bright. If the aggressive strategies required to rapidly expand the existing pool of experienced cruisers before there is an oversupply is implemented within the next few years, it will be smooth sailing through the temporary downturn of the early 1990s. Then the industry will be in an enviable position as the next century dawns. The potential for unprecedented success here reveals how important the anticipation of opportunities and threats is to the well-being of an entire industry. The foresight required to anticipate the temporary glut of ocean-going vessels and to recognize the opportunities the changing demographics and lower dollar represent is the fundamental asset any individual firm needs if it is to remain on top. The opportunities that exist for the cruise industry exist for other important service industries of the American economy. The will to make successes of these opportunities, however, requires the implementation of sound strategies that reflect the market conditions, international implications, and business savvy that have been too scarce in corporate America in the past.

10

THE SEMICONDUCTOR INDUSTRY: A CASE STUDY

The United States has held a position of dominance in high technology products since the Second World War. It has only been in recent years that this leadership position has been challenged by Japan and Europe (see Figure 10.1). More important, no other industrial sector has such political and economic significance as the semiconductor industry. It is no wonder, then, that with increasing competition from abroad many in the United States feel that Washington should take a more active role in preserving and protecting this sector. They fear that the United States is losing its competitive advantage as a result of unfair trade policies and the industrial targeting used by the governments of Japan and Europe. Many are afraid that just as the U.S. steel and auto industries fell from prominence in the 1960s and 1970s, so too will the U.S. semiconductor industry.

Due to its role as the foundation for other high tech products, the semiconductor industry is considered by many to be the most important of the high tech industries. Microchips are the building blocks of the information and automation revolution. Like steel, microchips are also the raw materials for other products, providing the computing and microprocessing power to an infinite number of products. They are increasingly being used in everyday items, such as toasters and refrigerators. They provide the "brains" to products ranging from ATMs to auto-

Figure 10.1
U.S. Semiconductor Shipments vs. World Shipments 1978–1987

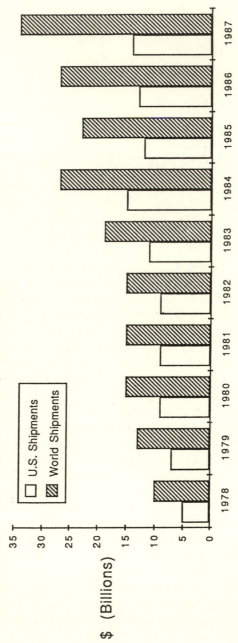

Source: Semiconductor Industry Association.

mobile fuel injection systems, from traffic signals to missile guidance systems.

To the businessman, a technological edge directly translates into a competitive edge. As semiconductors become increasingly common in products, more and more firms will depend on technological advances in this industry to achieve greater competitive advantages. With the advent of the information age, a firm's productivity depends on the quality of the tools it uses, such as telecommunication systems and computer systems, all of which rely heavily on advances in the semiconductor industry. There is great growth and profit potential in this industry for years to come, if for no other reason than as we become more dependent on technology and high tech products in our everyday life, we also become more dependent on the materials that make up these products.

Many experts feel that any nation wishing to be competitive in the twenty-first century must have a presence in the semiconductor industry. So compelling is this belief that many nations today already have governmental policies in place to subsidize and protect their developing seminconductor industries with the hope of assuring their survival and growth. For example, several European countries have bonded together in an ambitious project designed to overtake the United States and Japan in the international microchip and computer markets. Brazil has enacted some of the toughest trade legislation in an effort to protect its developing industries.

With increased competition from abroad and decreasing market shares, the United States has made several attempts to defend its technological leadership position in the semiconductor industry. Not surprisingly, most efforts have been targeted at Japan with the belief that Japan has achieved its success through unfair trade policies and pirated technology.

MARKET DYNAMICS

The key component that sets the semiconductor industry apart from other industries is the extremely rapid rate of technological change. Statistics show that on average the real cost of computing power is cut in half every few years. This translates to an industry characterized by very short product life cycles, high R&D costs, and constant change. The semiconductor industry is such a volatile industry that the major players of today may not even be around tomorrow. In fact, the major competitors in the semiconductor industry of the 1950s are no longer a factor in today's markets.

In 1956 RCA, Sylvania, and General Electric were among the leading electronic component makers in the United States, manufacturing vacuum tubes. New advances brought first transistor technology then integrated circuit technology. These established firms were overrun by small upstart companies like Fairchild and Motorola, who capitalized on the new markets the changing technology represented. They in turn were replaced by newcomers like Intel and National Semiconductor. The low-density, military-oriented chip producers of the 1960s were overrun by the medium-density, broad product-line firms of the 1970s. Today, these firms are being pushed out by the high-density, niche-market custom chip makers.

The pattern of change is evident in the semiconductor industry. Each time, the older, more established firm has grown too big and is unable or unwilling to respond to the changing technologies, it has been left behind. In this industry, a leadership position today does not guarantee a leadership position tomorrow. The corporate executive must be careful to remain responsive to the changing needs of the consumer and, more important, to identify and target maturing and developing strategic business sectors. It is in this way that a firm can stay abreast of technological advances and make sure that it is not left out in the cold.

The semiconductor industry, famous for its dynamic scale economies, is characterized by its extremely steep learning curves. A short product life cycle means that the cost of research and development cannot be amortized over many years. Thus, R&D costs become a large percentage of a firm's total costs. Product per unit costs are determined primarily through sales volume. Since in the semiconductor industry product life cycles are so short, most firms tend to be positioned on the steep portion of the learning curve. As product life cycles are extended, costs due to production/manufacturing improvements fall sharply.

It has been common in recent years to expect an electronic product introduced today to be available for less than half the price in just a few years. A good example of this is hand-held calculators. In the early 1970s, when these products were first being introduced to the consumer market, one could get a calculator that performed the basic addition, subtraction, multiplication, and division functions for about $70. With improvements in technology and in manufacturing processes an equivalent calculator can be purchased today for only a few dollars. In fact, for $20 one can get a fairly sophisticated scientific calculator that is about the size of a credit card.

In addition to dynamic scale economies, the semiconductor industry creates external economies that result from the spillover between firms. Some of the spillover resulting from personal contact leads to high tech industrial clusters, such as Route 128 in Massachusetts and the Silicon Valley area in California. Each of these high tech clusters exhibits similar environmental and economic structures that are already in place in the area.

The Silicon Valley, for example, is situated about forty miles south of San Francisco. This area is strategically situated within close proximity to three major metropolitan areas: San Francisco, Oakland, and San Jose. Its West Cost location allows for easy access to the Asian markets as well as U.S. markets, giving it an advantage in reduced transportation costs. It is also located near several major engineering and reseach schools, with Stanford University and the University of California at Berkeley being two of the more prestigious schools on the West Coast. The universities provide an incentive for firms to locate near them, due to their extensive research facilities and the highly trained workforce of scientists and engineers produced from each graduating class. Also, commercial spinoffs often result from research conducted within these universities. It is only a logical choice for ex-professors to set up shop in the area, making a commercial success of their research projects. Many other firms are drawn to this area by the strong military presence and their need for high tech products. Thus, these high tech industrial clusters are located in areas where economic, intellectual, and entrepreneurial conditions are strongest, making it a logical choice for firms to locate within the area.

THE U.S.–JAPANESE SEMICONDUCTOR INDUSTRY

Of major concern to the U.S. semiconductor industry is the Japanese semiconductor industry. In recent years, Japan has been acquiring a competitive advantage in areas in which the United States has traditionally been dominant. The main point of contention is that it has been a combination of government subsidies and the advantage of a protected domestic market, rather than market forces, that have lead to the rapid growth in Japanese semiconductor exports. The fear is that the United States is surrendering the semiconductor industry to the Japanese without a fight.

While it cannot be denied that direct government subsidies and a protected domestic market do contribute to a competitive advantage, it is uncertain as to the relative importance these "unfair" policies have had on the development of the Japanese semiconductor industry. Japan's targeting of the semiconductor industry has been one of the most documented and most successful examples of targeted industrial policies. This policy, spearheaded by the Ministry of International Trade and Industry (MITI), has been one of government subsidies, collaborative research among the firms within the industry, and the closure of their domestic chip market to outsiders. Beginning in the early 1970s, MITI convinced Japan's major industrial groups, or *kereitsu*, to accept a common strategy for catching up with the U.S. semiconductor industry. In return, MITI offered technical support, government subsidies, and market penetration via the closure of the domestic market.

With the semiconductor industry targeted, and under the guidance of MITI, firms such as Toshiba Corporation, Fujitsu Ltd., Hitachi Ltd., and Nippon Electric Corporation pooled their resources and expertise and worked together to overtake the U.S. competition in the race to develop the 64KB chip, the next generation of memory chips at the time. Japan prevented foreign companies from competing in its domestic market, thereby protecting its own companies and allowing them to develop. The Japanese firms were able to obtain cheap financing through Japan's large reserve of domestic savings. Early losses were absorbed by the larger companies and parent companies of the semiconductor firms, which were also their first largest customers. This provided the fledgling Japanese semiconductor firms with a ready-made, captive market. For example, Hitachi would get all of the chips it needed from its chip-making subsidy. This strategy paved the road toward a win-win situation for the Japanese semiconductor industry.

Financed and protected from the industry's market volatility, the Japanese chip-making firms were well prepared to penetrate world markets. From 1975 to 1985, these Japanese firms invested 35 percent of their sales into new plant and equipment, compared to 20 percent in the United States. So successful were the Japanese that by 1984 Japan held 70 percent of the world market for standardized microchips, and along the way became the most efficient and profitable chip makers in the world.

By mid-1985, the computer industry hit a slump and chip makers had an oversupply of inventory. The chip market was decreasing by more than 14 percent per year. The Japanese, however, continued producing chips and in an effort to maintain their market position began slashing prices. "In essence the Japanese were wrapping up a dollar bill or two with every chip and mailing it to the customer," says Texas Instruments spokesman Norman V. Neureiter.[1]

Within a year, the U.S. semiconductor industry was rapidly being driven out of its own markets. The White House charged the Japanese firms with "dumping," or selling their chips at discounted prices. Japanese firms, such as Hitachi, NEC, Toshiba, and Fujitsu, were accused of exporting chips to the United States at excessively low prices in order to maintain market share. As a result of continued pressures by the Reagan administration, a deal was reached in July 1986 whereby the Japanese would guarantee that chips exported to the United States would have a fair price, which would be determined by the U.S. Commerce Department. When that failed to work, the United States countered with trade sanctions in the form of $300 million in tariffs placed on Japanese electronic goods. Dumping slowed, but did not stop. Therefore, in April 1987, the United States imposed new sanctions, this time 100 percent duties on selected end products such as power tools and televisions. Pressured by these new sanctions, MITI was forced to impose export quotas to raise chip prices. This worked: chip prices rebounded, and most dumping sanctions were suspended by the United States in November 1987.

The net effect of the U.S.-Japan semiconductor trade accords of 1986 and 1987, however, was one of classic protectionism. Although prices were brought more in line with the fair market value, the trade agreement took away the incentive for Japanese chip makers to invest in plant expansion. The Japanese were able to sell their chips to the United States at higher prices, giving them a higher profit margin and the financing necessary to pursue expansion into other markets. This reduced supply created shortages and profit margins reached record highs. The Commerce Department, for example, estimates the average fair market value of a 256-kilobyte dynamic random-access memory chip, or 256K D-RAM, at less than $2, which includes profit margins. At the time the trade sanctions were put into effect, the Japanese were dumping these chips on the U.S. market at about $1 per chip. Today, large contract prices for chips have risen to $3 to $6 a chip, and spot-market prices are as high as $10 a chip, more than six times the cost of producing them. To be sure, this price distortion hurt U.S. industries that depended on these chips in their products. As with most trade sanctions, one industry is helped at the expense of another.

It is important to note that relative to the size of the industry, the size of the subsidies granted by MITI were not very large. The Semiconductor Industry Association estimates a total subsidy by MITI to the industry of $507 million from 1976 through 1982, which amounts to an average of $75 million per year. Japanese sales, however, in 1981 amounted to nearly $3 billion. Thus, the extent of the subsidies granted by MITI when measured as a percentage of total sales did not in and of themselves give the Japanese an unfair advantage. Also, the U.S. semiconductor industry receives billions of dollars each year from sales generated by American firms selling to government-financed programs which might also be considered a polite form of subsidization.

The difference between the U.S. and Japanese scenarios is the willingness of the Japanese government, banks, and a group of targeted companies to share the costs and the risks. The encouragement of joint research and market sharing allowed Japanese firms to avoid duplicate research, thus providing a more efficient use of research and development money and resources.

MARKET SUPPLY AND DEMAND

Helped greatly by the falling dollar against the yen, and backed by the trade agreements forced on Japan by the U.S. government, the U.S. semiconductor industry is looking healthier than it has in years. The industry is currently operating at a sales level of around $13 billion per year (see Figure 10.2), and semiconductor companies have returned to making a profit. Mergers are occurring at record rates as stronger companies broaden product lines by acquiring weaker ones. National Semiconductor's acquisition of Fairchild and Advanced Micro Devices's takeover of Monolithic Memories are both good examples.

What has happened in recent years in the industry is that Japan and the United States have solidified their market positions in their respective niches. The Japanese continue to control consumer electronics, while the United States leads in computers and the sophisticated microprocessors that go with them. The major players in the industry continue to be Japan and the United States, each controling about 43 percent of the $31 billion worldwide market for semiconductors. The other 14 percent is split among the European developed countries and the developing Asian ones, such as South Korea and Taiwan.

The semiconductor industry is expected to exhibit a continued growth rate of 13 to 14 percent per year for the next several years. Supply and demand conditions should remain on an even keel, with supplies remaining fairly abundant by past standards. Capacity constraints, except for advanced submicron components, should be rare. Product lead times—the length of

Figure 10.2
U.S. Semiconductor Sales 1984-1988

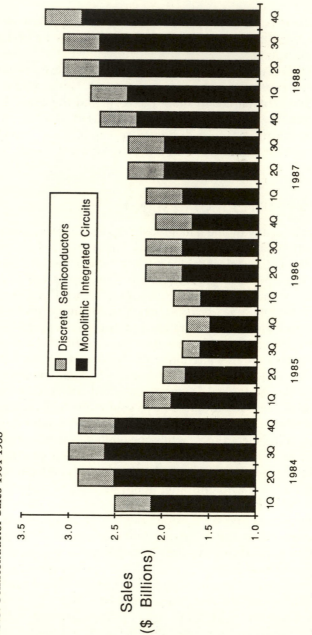

Source: Semiconductor Industry Association.

time between placement of an order and delivery—are not seen to be a significant problem. For instance, lead times for digital ICs in March 1988 were an average of nine weeks, as compared to a twenty-two-week lead time in 1984. The current relatively calm trade conditions and the stable growth rates will hold price increases to a minimum for digital bipolar, digital MOS, and linear ICs. Price increases will most likely remain in the 4 to 5 percent level.

COMPETITIVE TRADE STRATEGIES

It is obvious from the previous discussion that there will continue to be a healthy demand for semiconductors, if for no other reason than the fact that they serve as a primary raw material for so many products. As we move into the twenty-first century and the world becomes more technologically sophisticated, we will become increasingly dependent on high tech products and the components that make up these products. The question, then, is whether the international semiconductor markets will be shared among many nations, the United States included, or whether Japan will continue to gain market shares at the expense of U.S. firms. As other countries, such as the European community and developing countries, begin to gain access to the global semiconductor markets, competition for these market shares will only continue to increase and the U.S. share of these markets could continue to decline. Although the semiconductor industry has rebounded in recent years, mostly with the help of trade sanctions against Japan and the declining dollar, U.S. firms must develop strategies and put policies in place to continue to remain competitive in global markets.

Increasingly, the strategy for U.S. firms to regain market shares has been one of protectionist measures. This, however, must not be the case. The net effect of resolving the issue of Japanese dumping of chips in 1986 through trade sanctions, for example, has been disasterous for some industries. As previously mentioned, although these sanctions helped the semiconductor industry, they hurt other industries that are dependent on semiconductors. In fact, many in the computer industry consider U.S. semiconductor trade policy a total failure.

Even as late as the summer of 1988, many computer firms were upset by the fact that many chips it depended upon were in short supply and sold at inflated prices if and when they could be found. Angry at the high, inflated prices of 1 megabyte dynamic random-access memory chips (1MB DRAMs) and their scarce supply, Apple Computer accused Japanese suppliers of "malicious compliance" with the semiconductor agreement of 1986. It came down to the simple fact that Apple Computer was unable to obtain the 1MB DRAMs it needed for its Macintosh line of computers at a competitive price. According to Falcon Microsystems, Apple's government reseller, even Apple's key government customers were unable to get Macintosh II computers with more than 1MB of DRAM. As of June 1988, Falcon Microsystems still had 2,800 2MB memory boards on back order from Apple, with an estimated delivery date of over six months. The shortage of DRAMs had taken a toll on the availability of certain computers during a time when Apple was selling all the Macintoshes it could get out the door.

The danger of protectionism, as with this example, is one of artificially high prices and scarce supply. The computer industry needs these chips, and as a result is held hostage by the price necessary to obtain them. "We are searching for RAM the same way Apple and everybody else is—we just go on a bidding war," lamented Carlos Frum, president of Northbrook Computers. The net result of this form of protectionism is either lower profit margins for the firm, or higher prices for the consumer. In the end, everyone is hurt. "If you pay the price," says Frum, "you get the RAM . . . [and] some customers are beginning to realize they have to pay the price."[2]

FOCUSING ON STRENGTHS

The U.S. semiconductor industry must focus on its strengths to remain competitive in the future. The United States has long been characterized as a leader in innovation and superior in engineering skills and know-how. Firms must therefore develop strategies that complement their inherent strengths and natural advantages. The Japanese have achieved their competitive advantage by identifying a strategy of being the low-cost producer. They have done this by pouring large amounts of money into R&D, and into their plants and equipment, improving and perfecting their manufacturing processes along the way. Borrowing from U.S. manufacturing techniques developed in the 1960s and developing their own, the Japanese were able to become more productive, more efficient, and more quality conscious than any other firms in any other country. As a result of their efforts, they have made great strides in perfecting the mass production of memory chips, becoming the low-cost producer for many such products.

Market Focus

What U.S. firms must remember when developing strategies to compete in international markets is that most of their foreign compestititors are perfecting the manufacturing process of well-established and standard technology. They are simply moving down the manufacturing learning curve, realizing the economies of scale possible by applying mass-production techniques to these established products. It is also important to note that since a typical product life cycle in the semiconductor industry is so short (a few years at best), a competitive advantage of this type is likewise a short one. The rapid rate of technological change ensures that for a firm to remain competitive it must be at the forefront of new and developing technologies. In an industry characterized by continual change, the firm must either set the technological standard, be able to react quickly to changes in technology, or be left behind.

This is where the United States has its competitive advantage. The United States is well known and much admired for its entrepreneurial spirit, drive, and ingenuity. It is the entrepreneurs that built the Silicon Valleys of America and created the largest number of new jobs in recent years. In fact, the United States has seen the creation of over 113 semiconductor industries since 1977, while Japan has seen a total of only 4 (see Figure 10.3). In addition, of these start-ups, more than one-third have strong affiliations in the form of manufacturing contracts and joint ventures with Asian companies, many of them Japanese. Why play catch-up with the Japanese? We must put

Figure 10.3
Semiconductor Companies Formed Worldwide 1957–1986

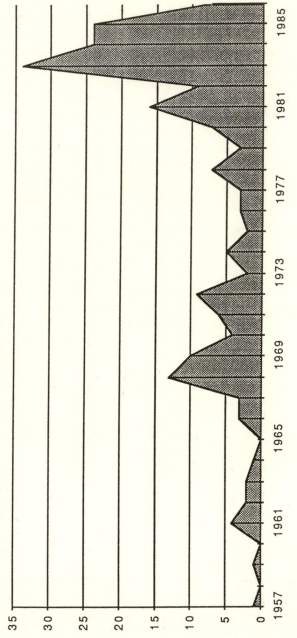

Source: Dataquest.

all our efforts into developing strategies that focus on the future, and do not dwell on the past. Just as Brazil may be better than the United States at making shoes, Japan and other countries may be better at manufacturing standardized chips. Their culture and economy may be better suited to this activity than the United States may ever be. Rather than protecting an industrial sector that may not be in our best interest to save, we should allow free trade to dictate which firms are competitive and which ones are not, thereby guaranteeing survival of the fittest.

Product Differentiation

A strategy well suited to the U.S. firm is that of product differentiation. By concentrating on developing new technologies and establishing market niches, the United States can sustain a competitive advantage. One sector of the industry in which the United States already has an inherent advantage is in designing and producing custom-made chips. The customized chip sector of the industry is expected to expand rapidly, accounting for more than 25 percent of total chip sales by 1990. These chips command prices of several thousands of dollars each, and engineering knowledge is more important than manufacturing efficiencies, since most of the product's value is obtained from the design of the chip itself. A competitive advantage in these chips is not obtained from mass-production techniques or cost cutting, but rather from the engineering skills and talent required to design these custom chips.

The United States has a natural competitive advantage in this sector, since most of the world's top chip designers are Americans, as are most of the leading software writers, who tell these custom chips what to do. Unlike the production and shipping of standardized memory chips, this industry requires a continual dialogue with the customer during the design and development phase. As such, the United States has a language, location, and cultural advantage in this sector.

Finally, due to its characteristics of being knowledge intensive and requiring low overhead, the customized chip sector and other such market niches are naturals in attracting U.S.

entrepreneurs and venture capitalists. Cypress Semiconductor Corporation, for example, a relatively new, small-sized start-up firm in the Silicon Valley area, is already doing amazingly well dealing exclusively in these chips.

SEMATECH

The recent formation of Sematech, the semiconductor industry research consortium, is a major step forward in addressing and resolving weaknesses in the industry. Many consider this joint venture between the semiconductor industry and the U.S. government vital if the United States is to stay competitive with Japan, and MITI is an excellent example of the achievements possible through government-aided industrial targeting. The key issue, then, is in Sematech's implementation.

The group's current goal is to develop state-of-the-art chipmaking techniques with exclusively U.S. materials by 1993. Sematech must emphasize the coordination of research minds and dollars to pursue new technologies and manufacturing processes. MITI's success came from the efficient use of its limited resources and the promotion of targeted industries that had future promise. Sematech would do well to follow their example. The aim so far, however, has been to improve the manufacturing process as opposed to the engineering process. Rather than developing manufacturing techniques that will compete with current processes, Sematech's budget would be better spent promoting and developing manufacturing processes of the type needed to quickly turn out small batches of one-of-a-kind products, such as customized chips. Sematech must also form alliances with universities and work with them to develop the new technologies required for future commercial products. The role of Sematech is that of a coordinator. It must be careful to make sure that it does not create a bureaucracy of sorts that will stifle the creativity and the entrepreneurialism necessary in this industry.

U.S. firms must decide what business they are in and what their competitive strategy will be. If a firm chooses to be a low-cost producer, it must look at ways of improving the manufacturing process. The corporate executive would do well to support design standardization and product standardization among the chip-making firms. This will aid in decreasing product development times and allow different products to communicate with each other. If a firm chooses to be an innovator, it must obtain the best engineers it can find who will successfully develop the technologies of the future. Firms must make alliances with universities, promoting cooperative education programs that allow college students to obtain internships. Firms must make a commitment to R&D activities, continually examining new technologies and determining whether they represent future markets. Customized chips are only one such sector that shows promise. Recent advances in superconductor research and new chip architectures, such as the RISC architecture, may prove to be the markets of the future. The formation of Sematech will only serve to strengthen the industry, eliminating unnecessary duplication of effort among engineering firms, and establishing a target much in the same way the MITI does in Japan. The future for the U.S. semiconductor industry is a bright one, provided that the necessary steps are taken to allow firms to build on their strengths and develop sustainable competitive advantages.

NOTES

1. Rusty Weston and Rory J. O'Connor, "Apple Insists DRAM Pact Must Change," *Macintosh Today*, June 13, 1988.

2. Holman Jenkins, Jr., "Chip War Success a Dubious Model for U.S. Policy," *Insight*, May 2, 1988.

11

SUMMARY

The dramatic decline in American preeminence in the world economic arena is a direct result of the emergence of other nations, most notably West Germany and Japan, as economic powerhouses in their own right. The traditional ability of the United States to "impose its will" as it so splendidly did in the aftermath of the Second World War has eroded, for the world community is comprised of nations that are more equal than in years past. The natural renegotiation of the dilemma of trade has contributed to the economic dislocation of the past decade as well as encouraged reactionary protectionist sentiment in this country. The observed response, while understandable, has a more insidious side, for it both encourages protectionist legislation that invites retaliation and it promotes misguided ideas, such as those embodied in arguments in favor of "tailored" trade. The consequences of both these developments endanger the long-term prospects of the American economy.

If corporate America is to enjoy a sustainable competitive advantage in the global economy it will do so through a program that focuses on America's strengths: productivity and technological innovation. The resolution to the dilemma of trade among equals benefits both parties. In order, however, for the optimal outcome to prevail, both parties must negotiate from a position of strength. The task for the executive manager is to strengthen his firm, for in so doing the economic base of the nation is strengthened, as is the negotiating position. The undeniable role of productivity in meeting the challenges at hand cannot be underestimated. To a great extent productivity is tied to the internal organizational structure and resource allocation within firms. The horizontal management structure that harnesses the benefits of economies of scale and scope is vital if the corporate entity is to improve productivity and its competitive position.

The discussion presented here, moreover, has alluded to the limitations faced by the corporation. While there are strategic decisions that must be implemented by each firm, external factors, such as legislation and devaluations, contribute to the success or the frustration encountered. For the executive the implication is clear: while he may have no direct control over a given factor, he must attempt to influence it. To this end, corporate America would be well served by a program promoting adherence to the rules of GATT, the adoption of stable exchange rates, a reduction of protectionist measures among the industrialized nations, and support for programs that facilitate the implementation of the high technology measures that increase productivity.

The economic dislocation the United States has suffered, coupled with the inability to resolve the federal and trade deficit crises, has further weakened America's bargaining position. In much the same way that Japan benefits from a suboptimal outcome at the expense of the United States, more nations in the future will be in a position to "impose" such outcomes. This is not to say that there are not opportunities for building momentum and regaining lost ground. The service and high technology sectors hold vast and unfulfilled promise for corporate America. As the two case studies demonstrated, the cruise industry and the high tech semiconductor industry are but two areas where the United States can profit from long-term sustainable competitive advantages in the global marketplace. There are ample opportunities in the information, manufacturing, and services components of the salariat economy that constitute the mechanism for building a prosperous future.

Whether this potential is realized, however, remains to be seen. It will depend on whether corporate America can implement the strategies necessary to develop higher productivity gains and Washington can promote international cooperation through the amplification of GATT and the stabilization of exchange rates and fiscal policies. These tasks go hand in hand. The future lies in trade and those who are able to participate in the global economy in a rigorous way. To be sure, only firms in a position of weakness seek the kind of protection so eagerly sought by myopic managers. However many are wont to seek protectionism, it is clear that these are misguided calls that would produce only short-term benefits. Even more threatening to the international economy are arguments made in favor of dismantling GATT. Although there are shortcomings in the administration of GATT which are of no small consequence, efforts must be focused on widening GATT and not eliminating it. No rational alternative exists for the promotion of trade. The interests of corporate America lie in securing more open markets overseas. If, as is almost certain, foreign firms will not withdraw from the American market, the only option is to learn to compete. Corporate America stands to benefit from the implementation of programs to compete at home and abroad. How America is to regain lost power without competing in the global marketplace is unclear. Real economic growth lies in achieving a sustainable competitive advantage that delivers success in both domestic and foreign markets. Indeed, as corporate America becomes more competitive, the position of the United States is strengthened, as is the world economy. Success lies in no other course. The dilemma of trade must be resolved so that the optimal outcome prevails, for no other possibility would avert a crisis.

APPENDIXES

1

The General Agreement on Tariffs and Trade

The General Agreement on Tariffs and Trade (GATT) was initially ratified in Geneva by twenty-three participating countries on October 30, 1947. It remains today the only international trade agreement with over ninety country members that together account for 80 percent of all world trade. As such, it has had the power and capability over the years to shape and influence the international economy. A 300-member GATT secretariat, based in Geneva, provides a forum for the airing of trade disputes among member nations, giving GATT a mediator role in world trade disputes. It also coordinates committees on special trade issues and monitors compliance with trade agreements.

The main provisions of GATT were designed to prevent the protectionist sentiments that led to the serious trade wars of the 1930s. They are as follows:

1. Member nations must give a most favored nation (MFN) status to its other members, allowing equal nondiscriminatory access to their domestic markets. The purpose was to prevent selective retaliatory measures and countermeasures between countries. For example, if country A grants country B MFN status, then country A cannot give country C better terms of trade than it does country B. Thus if country A cuts tariffs on country B, it must also make an equal tariff cut on country C.

2. Import quotas and other transparent forms of tariffs are not permitted, unless when necessary to protect domestic production control programs or to prevent a balance of trade crisis.

3. Once tariffs have been removed or reduced, they must not be reimposed in the form of compensatory domestic taxes, such as levying a higher excise tax on imports than on similar domestic products.

4. Where imports are shown to threaten domestic industries producing similar items, member nations may impose countervailing tariffs to offset this threat. Also, an escape clause allows for a suspension or modification of agreed-upon concessions when a surge of imports threatens domestic industries.

Under GATT, the main instrument in securing trade agreements is through negotiations at tariff bargaining conferences. Seven major conferences have been held since GATT's inception, with the most recent rounds taking place in Uruguay. In the early conferences, the main method of negotiation involved a principal supplier of a product in a specific market requesting concessions from the importer. If and when the two sides agreed on a mutually advantageous arrangement, it was generalized to all other GATT members via the MFN provision. This ensured that all participants would benefit from trade liberalization, since there is no obligation to agree to concessions unless they are mutually beneficial, and everyone will gain advantages as a by-product from other countries' concessions.

The gains in trade liberalization since GATT was founded are impressive. Tariffs have fallen from average levels of 30 to 50 percent at the end of the Second World War to averages as low as 4 to 5 percent in the major industrialized countries. Today, world trade in manufactured goods has fewer obstacles than at any other time in history. Both the Dillon (1960–1961) and the Kennedy (1964–1967) rounds of negotiations cut tariffs on manufactured goods by approximately 25 percent. The Tokyo (1973–1979) rounds cut tariffs by almost 30 percent. In addition, the volume of trade has increased more than seven times since 1950. MFN status has been extended to include many other countries. Several hundred additional bilateral agreements have been put into operation via these negotiation rounds.

2

Theory of Nontariff Barriers

In economic terms, a nontariff barrier (NTB) is a regulation on trade other than a tariff that is imposed by a government and that directly alters the quantity or patterns of trade. NTBs have long been thought to be a more harmful method of restricting trade, and efforts have been made by GATT to restrict their use. The problem, however, lies in the fact that GATT has no power to enforce its policies and rules. GATT is only as good as its members allow it to be. Thus, despite GATT's efforts to eliminate them in every round of trade negotiations, NTBs have remained and are increasingly being used by individual nations as an integral trade policy tool. Given the pattern of increased use of NTBs, it is important to understand the theoretical significance of NTBs and the economic difference between NTBs and tariff-based barriers.

Quantitative restrictions, such as import quotas, are an example of an NTB. In the simplest sense, import quotas are similar to a tariff. Placing an import quota, for example, on Japanese automobiles reduces the supply of these cars. This in turn causes imports to be more expensive than comparably equipped U.S. cars, making them less attractive than their U.S. equivalents. A tariff, on the other hand, directly increases the price of the foreign competition by tacking an import fee onto the price of the car, making it more expensive. This is most easily shown by the supply and demand curve in Figure A.1. The

Figure A.1
Economic Effects of Nontariff Barriers

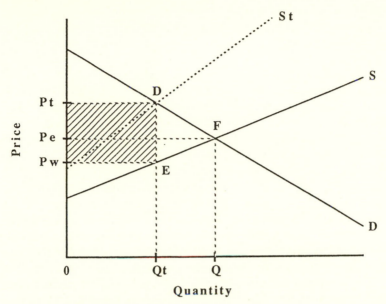

Source: All appendix figures prepared by International Credit Monitor.

supply and demand for an imported product are shown by lines S and D. Assuming that domestic supply is omitted in this discussion, the free-trade equilibrium level is given by point F. This is the level at which supply and demand are balanced, and free trade dictates a quantity, Q, to be produced and sold at a price of P_e.

Suppose that a quantitative restriction, Q_o, is placed on the product. Since this restriction is less than the demand for the product on the free market, the domestic price increases. Effectively, the domestic demand is still at point F while the supply has been artificially limited. The domestic price increases to point P_t, allowing the global price of the import to decrease to the value at point P_w.

Since the amount of a tariff separates the domestic from the global price of the import, a tariff rate must be equal to the percentage by which it increases the internal price of the product over the external price. Therefore, a quota that produces a price distortion of P_tP_w/P_wO is equivalent in its restrictive effect to a tariff of that given percentage increase. In Figure A.1 the supply curve S_t indicates the equivalent tariff schedule that reflects the domestic price and tariff that must be paid for the import.

What makes an NTB as a trade control tool more harmful than an equivalent tariff is its political and economic ramifications. Politically, an NTB is more palatable than a tariff. For example, it is much easier for a U.S. automobile manufacturer to secure from Congress a 2.3 million-unit quota on Japanese cars than it is to convince them of an import tax of, say, 50 percent. Congress would consider such a tariff excessively high and would object. Also, the public can well understand the tariff or import tax that suddenly makes the cost of a product more expensive. However, few consumers if any would be able to compute the equivalent tariff rate on an NTB. Thus, an NTB allows an excessively high tariff to be hidden behind the guise of an import quota or voluntary restriction.

The economic effects of an NTB are greater distortions to the free flow of trade, since these barriers are generally restrictive in nature. In economic terms, with growth, the supply and demand curves shift to the right to reflect a greater demand for a product. As demand increases, if an import quota remains constant, the equivalent tariff rate continues to increase, passing a greater cost burden to the consumer. At least with a tariff, it would remain constant and economies of scale would help to lower the price of the good.

If demand for a product increases or the supply increases due to productivity gains, the optimal quantity of imports also increases. A tariff would permit this to happen, but an NTB would not. As one can see, an NTB destroys the sensitivity of the market to any economic change that calls for more imports. In effect, it destroys the free flow of trade and hinders market efficiencies.

Of some significance is the lost revenue an NTB over a tariff represents to the federal government. A tariff produces income. In Figure A.1, the shaded rectangle P_tP_wED represents the income generated by a tariff for the government, due to the artificial price increase effects of a trade barrier. In the case of an NTB, this represents lost revenue, since a quota produces no income for the government. However, the privilege to sell a product on the U.S. market at an inflated price of P_t and the option to sell at a deflated price of P_w in the global marketplace is of value to a foreign producer.

From the figure we can see that the equilibrium price level of the product is at a price below P_t, while the global marketplace commands a price of P_w. Because of this price advantage, the government is able to auction off licences for the privilege to import goods at an inflated price into the United States to the highest bidder. If this privilege is given away, these proceeds, in effect, go to the importer. Not only do these barriers from trade provide higher profit margins on the U.S. market, but they give foreign firms an inherent competitive advantage in price over their U.S. competitors and the means of expanding market share on an international level. This hinders the ability of U.S. firms to compete with their foreign counterparts in the global marketplace. In economics, the world welfare cost of restriction is determined by the triangle DEF.

In many instances, an import quota serves only to harm the industry it is trying to protect. In the case of the automobile industry, placing quotas on Japanese imports in the early 1980s allowed Japanese competitors to concentrate on higher priced cars that generated a higher profit margin. U.S. automakers were slow to adjust and react to the changing market demands for larger, more luxurious autos, just as they were slow to provide smaller, more fuel-efficient autos during the oil crisis in the 1970s. Competing producers favor quotas, since they protect against future uncertainty in the economy that would lead to any increase in a competitor's imports. By relying on import quotas and trade barriers, many U.S. firms have jeopardized their future for the safety of the present.

3

Gains from Trade

The most basic theory of trade is that of gains from trade, first observed by John Stuart Mill in his *Principles of Political Economy* (1848) and later by David Ricardo. This fundamental proposition is stated as follows: "If in the absence of trade relative prices of commodities differ between countries, countries can gain by exchanging commodities at intermediate price ratios."[1]

We can demonstrate this by considering a two-country model, in which each country is "endowed" with a given quantity of food and clothing and cannot alter that quantity. Figure A.2 shows what is commonly referred to by economists as the "trade triangle" for the home country. Curves y_0 and y_1 represent two indifference curves, which express individual preferences for food and clothing. An individual is considered to be "indifferent" to any mix of food and clothing that lies on a given indifference curve. In effect, the individual obtains the same level of satisfaction from any combination of food and clothing on that curve.

Point E represents the aggregate bundle of food and clothing available to the home country in the absence of any trade. It is obvious that any point northeast of point E, such as point F, is preferred to point E's mix of goods, since it will have a greater aggregate bundle of goods than point E has. Likewise, any point southwest of point E, such as point I, must be less desirable.

Two budget lines are drawn through point E, each repre-

Figure A.2
Gains from Trade: The Trade Triangle for the Home Country

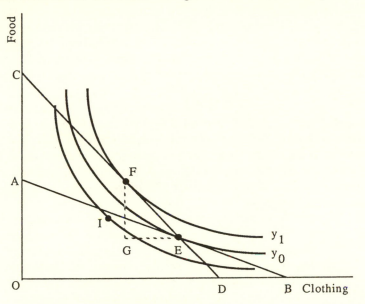

In the absence of trade, the home country consumes a given bundle of food and clothing as defined by point E, and at a relative price shown by the slope of line AB. If it could trade at prices shown by line CD, it would export GE units of clothing and import FG units of food, thereby consuming a more favorable bundle of goods at point F.

senting a different relative price of food/clothing, with food being relatively cheaper along line CED than along line AEB. For each relative price level, and its associated budget line, there is a consumption preference point if the community can exchange its goods at the given price. For example, point F is the pre-ferred consumption point along budget line CED. All other points lie on lower indifference curves relative to point F.

The key to this discussion is that the bundle of goods defined by point F *cannot* be consumed if the country is not allowed to trade with other nations, since point E is the maximum mix of commodities available to the home country. It would be forced to consume food and clothing only in the amounts locally avail-able.

Line CED, then, illustrates the possibilities open to this country to trade at relative prices different from those prevailing before trade. It could offer to export GE units of clothing in exchange for the same value of food (FG). Such a trade would allow the country to consume the bundle of goods defined by point F, which lies on a more preferred indifference curve than does point E. Using this same argument, the reverse is shown to be true for the other country.

We can thus prove that the opportunity to trade at relative prices different from those in isolation must improve real incomes at home. Although the total supply of food and clothing remains fixed, due to our fixed endowment assumption, a redistribution of each commodity from the country in which it is cheaper to the country in which it is more expensive is beneficial to both countries.

NOTE

1. John Stuart Mill, *Principles of Political Economy*, vol. 2 (New York: P. F. Collier and Son, 1900), p. 96.

4

Free-Trade Equilibrium

Free-trade equilibrium refers to the notion that there is a common relative price ratio at which two countries can mutually benefit from trade. Free trade implies that there is a world market in which a common price is established for a given commodity. Supply and demand curves are used to establish that such an equilibrium can be obtained, and therefore exists. Figure A.3 shows the combined home and foreign supply and demand curves for a single commodity, food.

We assume a fixed, combined supply of food: $S_{F1} + S_{F2}$. We further assume that the relative price of food is cheaper abroad than at home. The higher price, OP_1, indicates the price that would clear the home market if it did not trade. Conversely, price OP_2 represents the price that would clear the foreign markets. Since food is more expensive at home than abroad, the home country would be willing to purchase food from abroad at the lower price OT. Likewise, the foreign country would be willing to sell its excess food at price OT, because of the profit it would realize in the sale, as indicated by P_2T. The world market is cleared at the intermediate equilibrium price level of OT.

Figure A.3
Free-Trade Equilibrium: World Supply and Demand Curves

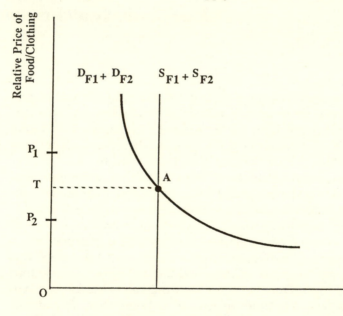

The free-trade equilibrium price level, OT, is determined by the equilibrium between the world demand for food (curve D) and the world supply of food (curve S).

5

Efficiency of Competition

Competition promotes the efficient allocation of resources. Barriers to trade, such as voluntary export restraints (VERs), tariffs, and other protectionist measures inhibit competition, since they artificially restrict trade. Free trade, however, encourages competition.

To demonstrate that there is an efficiency of competition, consider a world with only two commodities: food and clothing. Also in this world, there are only two production factors: labor and capital. Figure A.4 shows arbitrarily chosen isoquants for the food and clothing industries. Isoquant curves F_1 and F_2 represent two possible production levels for food. Each point on the isoquant curve represents a different quantity of labor and capital needed to produce a given quantity of food. Thus points A and B on isoquant F_1 each represent two different mixes of labor and capital that will guarantee a level of output as defined by F_1. Also, isoquant F_1 is associated with a higher level of production than is isoquant F_2. The same holds true for the isoquants that describe two possible clothing production levels, C_1 and C_2.

Line DAE is a constant-factor cost line for the mix of labor and capital as defined by point A. The slope of line DAE reflects the ratio of the wage rate to the rental on capital equipment. The efficiency of competition assures that each industry will choose a labor/capital mix so that at that production point

Figure A.4
Efficiency of Competition

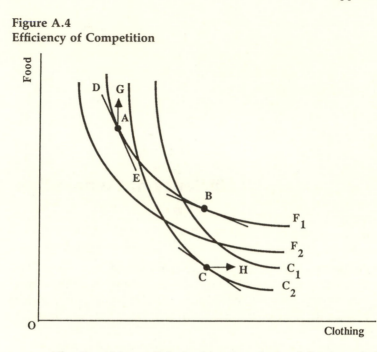

Allocating a labor-capital mix of A units to food and C units to clothing
is inefficient. An equal transfer of labor to clothing (arrow CH) and
capital to food (arrow AG) serves to raise outputs in both industries.

each isoquant has the same slope. It is at this point that there
is an efficient allocation of resources.

For example, points A and C represent two production points,
one for food production and the other for clothing production.
The slopes of the isoquants at points A and C are unequal. If
the clothing industry is able to take some labor from the food
industry and give it some of its capital, as shown by arrows
AG and CH, then both industries could achieve greater productivity. This is because point G lies above the food isoquant's
initial point A, and point G lies above the clothing isoquant's
initial point B. The total resources used by the economy are the
same, since an equal amount of labor and capital was ex-
changed. Therefore, there will continue to be an exchange of
labor and capital until the optimal mix is achieved and the slopes
of the two production points are equal.

Competition assures that resources will be allocated efficiently since in each industry the decision as to which manufacturing technique to use is based on cost considerations. That is, the choice of manufacturing techniques is determined in an attempt to minimize costs. Just as an individual consumer minimizes the cost of obtaining a given level of real income by choosing a point at which his indifference curve is tangential to his budget line, so too will a cost-conscious firm select the most economical combination of labor and capital. This is accomplished by selecting the point of tangency between an isoquant and a constant-factor cost line. If both firms face the same wage rates for labor and interest rates on capital, as in the case of competitive markets, then the marginal rate of substitution equals the common wage rate/interest rate ratio. In this way, competition ensures that the conditions for an efficient allocation of resources are met.

6

Comparative Advantage

A country is said to have a comparative advantage in a given commodity over another country if its relative price is lower at home before trade. This indicates that it is cheaper to produce the commodity at home than elsewhere. This may be due to any number of reasons, such as more efficient production methods, lower labor costs, or easier access to raw materials.

In general, positions of comparative advantage are based on both the desire, or demand, for the product and the conditions of production, or supply. Figure A.5 illustrates the comparison between the supply and demand for a given product, such as food. We assume that there is a strong demand but a weak supply of food at home. This causes food to be relatively more expensive at home than abroad. By showing quantities of food relative to quantities of clothing we can ignore factors that might influence pretrade prices, such as a country's size, or its relative power position. Pretrade supply and demand are shown by curves D and S. If there is a greater demand for food at home than abroad and a surplus of food abroad, then trade will permit the supply and demand to be represented by curves S_T and D_T. The demand for food at home is allowed to increase, and trade permits a greater supply of food. As a result, food prices decrease from a pretrade price of OA to a price of OA_T. This indicates that the trading country has a comparative advantage in food production.

Figure A.5
Comparative Advantage: Relative Demands and Supplies

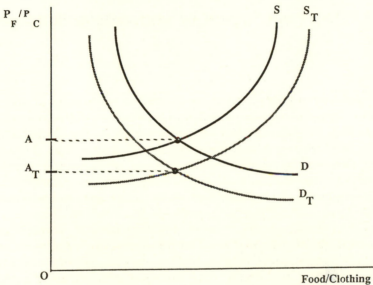

A relatively strong demand and relatively weak supply of food at home make food more expensive at home. This is shown by the fact that in the absence of trade the price of food (OA) is more expensive than when trade exists between nations (OA_T).

7

The Importance of Technology to Trade

Technology and its products are important components of trade, accounting for over 30 percent of U.S. manufacturers' exports. The U.S. Department of Commerce identifies a high technology industry as one that possesses two characteristics: 1) it has an above-average level of scientists and engineers (a highly trained workforce), and 2) it has a rapid rate of technological development. What makes this sector unique over other industrial sectors is its strategic importance to a country.

Government agencies have traditionally been a major source of funding for high tech product development. The reason for this is simple. Most new technology has its roots in military applications. The United States, for example, has maintained its lead in commercial technology primarily through spin-offs from military research and the space program (NASA). Advances in aircraft technology, computer science, and microchip technology have often been due to military needs that directly led to commercial applications. As a result, a technological lead is usually considered of interest to national security and a measure of a country's military potential. In fact, this is a commonly used argument in favor of protectionist legislation. Many lawmakers and industrial leaders have warned that the high technology industry is too important to our national interest to allow it to deteriorate any further.

Due to its very nature, then, a presence in the high tech industry has also become a symbol of economic power. Just as in the 1950s a national presence in steel was a political must for any country that could afford it, so too is the high tech industry in the 1980s and 1990s. Only the most advanced countries are capable of possessing the skills and resources necessary to compete in this sector. "If you are state-of-the-art in high technology," says Michael Borrus, deputy director of the Berkeley Roundtable on the International Economy at the University of California, "you will be state-of-the-art in everything else . . . from agriculture to manufacturing, from aircrafts to selling insurance."[1]

Many countries today are following the examples of the United States and Japan, believing that success in technology will bring power, prosperity, and a higher standard of living. Traditional processes of NIC (newly industrialized country) development, providing agricultural or low tech products to the industrialized countries, are being abandoned in favor of establishing a presence in a high tech industry. Increasingly, these countries are jumping on the high tech bandwagon. "Countries that make airplanes and electronics have greater geopolitical power than countries that grow wheat and cut down trees," says Clyde V. Prestowitz, a former Reagan administration trade official. "It's that simple."[2]

NOTES

1. Holman Jenkins, Jr., "Chip War Success a Dubious Model for U.S. Policy," *Insight*, May 2, 1988, p. 12.
2. Holman Jenkins, Jr., "Awakening to Loss in High-tech Lead," *Insight*, May 2, 1988, p. 8.

>

BIBLIOGRAPHY

Aho, M. C., and J. D. Aroson, *Trade Talks*. New York: Council of Foreign Relations, 1985.

Ansoff, H. Igor. "The Firm of the Future." *Harvard Business Review* (September-October 1965).

Bergsten, C. F., and W. R. Cline. *Trade Policy in the 1980s*. Washington, D.C.: Institute for International Economics, 1983.

Bhagwati, J. N. *Import Competition and Response*. Chicago: University of Chicago Press, 1982.

Boyatizis, Richard. *The Competent Manager*. New York: Wiley, 1981.

Caves, Richard E., and Ronald W. Jones. *World Trade and Payments*. Boston: Little, Brown & Company, 1981.

Choate, Pat, and Juyne Linger. "Tailored Trade: Dealing with the World as It Is," *Harvard Business Review* (January-February 1988).

Cline, William *Trade Policy in the 1980s*. Washington, D.C.: Institute for International Economics, 1983.

Council of Economic Advisers. *Annual Report*. Washington, D.C.: U.S. Government Printing Office, 1983.

———. *Annual Report*, Washington, D.C.: U.S. Government Printing Office, 1987.

Drucker, Peter F. *Technology, Management and Society*. New York: Heinemann, 1970.

———. *Managing in Turbulent Times*. London: Heinemann, 1980.

———. *The Changing World of the Executive*. New York: Time Books, 1982.

Eckelmann, R., and L. Davis. *Japanese Industrial Policies and the Development of High Technology Industries: Computers and Aircraft*.

Washington, D.C.: U.S. Department of Commerce, Office of Trade and Investment Analysis, 1983.

Farnsworth, Clyde H. "U.S. Contractors Win Role in Japan Projects." *New York Times*, March 30, 1988.

Frank, Robert H. *Choosing the Right Pond: Human Behavior and the Quest for Status*. New York: Oxford University Press, 1985.

Galbraith, John Kenneth, *The New Industrial State*. Harmondsworth: Penguin Books, 1968.

————. *The Affluent Society*. 2d ed. Boston: Houghton Mifflin, 1969.

————. *Economics in Perspective*. Boston: Houghton Mifflin, 1977.

Grayson, C. Jackson, Jr., and Carla O'Dell. *American Business: A Two-Minute Warning*. New York: The Free Press, 1988.

Jenkins, Holman, Jr., "Chip War Success a Dubious Model for U.S. Policy." *Insight* (May 2, 1988).

Kennedy, Paul. *The Rise and Fall of the Great Powers*. New York: Random House, 1987.

Krauss, M. B. *The New Protectionism: The Welfare State and International Trade*. New York: New York University Press, 1978.

Kreinin, M. E. *International Economics: A Policy Approach*. 4th ed. New York: Harcourt Brace Jovanovich, 1983.

Krugman, P. *U.S. Response to Foreign Industrial Targeting, Brookings Papers on Economic Activity*. Washington, D.C.: Brookings Institution, 1984.

Kusumoto, Sam. "Manager's Journal." *The Wall Street Journal*, March 14, 1988.

Landau, Ralph. "U.S. Economic Growth." *Scientific American* 358, no. 6 (June 1988).

Lang, H. Jack. *Letters in American History: Words to Remember*. New York: Harmony Books, 1982.

Magaziner, I., and R. Reich. *Minding America's Business*. New York: Vintage Books, 1982.

McKenzie, Richard. "Textile Gripes Are Made of Whole Cloth," *The Wall Street Journal*, April 8, 1988.

McKinnon, R. I. *An International Standard for Monetary Stabilization*. Washington, D.C.: Institute for International Economics, 1984.

Mill, John Stuart. *Principles of Political Economy*. Vol. 2. New York: P. F. Collier and Son, 1900.

Modelski, George. *Transnational Corporations and World Order: Readings in International Political Economy*. San Francisco: W. H. Freeman, 1979.

Morkre, Morris E. *Import Quotas on Textiles: The Welfare Effects of United States Restrictions on Hong Kong*. Bureau of Economics Staff Report to the Federal Trade Commission. Washington, D.C.: U.S. Government Printing Office, 1984.

Newcomb, Wilbur. American Textile International.

Nixon, Richard M. *1999: Victory Without War*. New York: Simon and Schuster, 1988.

Orwell, George. *Animal Farm*. New York: New American Library, 1974.

Osmond, Neville. "Top Management: Its Tasks, Roles and Skills." *Journal of Business Policy* (Winter 1971).

Peters, Thomas J., and Robert H. Waterman. *In Search of Excellence*. New York: Harper & Row, 1988.

Porter, Michael E. *Competitive Strategy: Techniques for Analyzing Industries and Competitors*. New York: The Free Press, 1980.

———. *Competitive Advantage: Creating and Sustaining Superior Performance*. New York: The Free Press, 1985.

Potts, Mark, and Behr Peter. *The Leading Edge*. New York: McGraw-Hill, 1987.

Reischauer, Edwin O. *The United States and Japan*. Cambridge: Harvard University Press, 1980.

———. *Japan, The Story of a Nation*, 3d ed. New York: Alfred A. Knopf, 1981.

Sahal, D. *Patterns of Technological Innovation*. Reading, Mass.: Addison-Wesley, 1981.

Salvatore, Dominick. *The New Protectionist Threat to World Welfare*. New York: North-Holland, 1987.

Schelling, Thomas. *Micromotives and Macrobehavior*. New York: W. W. Norton, 1978.

Scott, B. R., and G. C. Lodge. *U.S. Competitiveness in the World Economy*. Boston: Harvard Business School Press, 1986.

Semiconductor Industry Association. *The Effect of Government Targeting on World Semiconductor Competition*. Washington, D.C., 1983.

Silk, Leonard, "Economic Scene." *New York Times*, April 1, 1988.

Thurow, Lester. *Zero Sum Solution*. New York: Simon and Schuster, 1985.

U.S. Congress. House Committee on Energy and Commerce, 1985.

U.S. Department of Commerce. *An Assessment of U.S. Competitiveness in High Technology Industries*. February, 1985.

Verdoorn, P. J. *Fattori che regolano lo sviluppo della produttivita del lavoro*. *L'Industria*, 1949.

Waldman, Peter. "Sematech Rushes to Meet Japan Challenge." *Wall Street Journal*, January 8, 1988.

Weber, Max. *Max Weber on Law in Economy and Society*. Cambridge: Harvard University Press, 1954.

Weston, Rusty, and Rory J. O'Connor. "Apple Insists DRAM Pact Must
    Change." *Macintosh Today*, June 13, 1988.
World Bank, *World Development Report, 1988*. New York: Oxford Uni-
    versity Press.

>>

INDEX

LOUIS E. V. NEVAER is Director of Political Analysis at International Credit Monitor, a consulting firm specializing in political risk assessments, of which he is co-founder. He has extensive experience in overseas work, and has worked as a consultant to foreign governments and international firms. He is the author of the POP curve, a macroeconomic tool useful in understanding the national debt capacity of an economy as well as determining the point of diminishing returns of government debt. He and Steven Deck are the coauthors of *Corporate Financial Planning and Management in a Deficit Economy* (Quorum Books, 1987) and *The Management of Corporate Business Units: Portfolio Strategies for Turbulent Times* (Quorum Books, 1988).

STEVEN A. DECK is Executive Director of Data and Statistical Analysis at International Credit Monitor, of which he is co-founder. He has worked for, and more recently consulted to multinational companies specializing in information systems, project tracking, and financing. With Mr. Nevaer, he is the coauthor of *Corporate Financial Planning and Management in a Deficit Economy* (Quorum Books, 1987) and *The Management of Corporate Business Units: Portfolio Strategies for Turbulent Times* (Quorum Books, 1988).